The Esthetic of Jean Cocteau

The Esthetic of Jean Cocteau

Lydia Crowson

Published for The University of New Hampshire
by The University Press of New England
Hanover, New Hampshire 1978

Published with assistance from
the Andrew W. Mellon Foundation

**The University Press
of New England**

Brandeis University
Clark University
Dartmouth College
University of New Hampshire
University of Rhode Island
University of Vermont

Contents

Introduction

So many books have been written about Jean Cocteau that one might question the reasons for yet another. Implicit in previous studies is the assumption that Cocteau's art represents an aberration in the history of French letters because it manifests contradictory characteristics drawn from surrealism, cubism, the Boulevard, and cabaret theater. Since the work does not lend itself to traditional types of literary categorization, the impression left by most critics is that some individual pieces are cleverly conceived but the opus as a whole lacks coherence and significance.

In this context it should be noted that no major study of Cocteau has been based on the critical tools made available through the research of structuralists (Goldmann and Ricardou, for example) or on the methodology associated with analytic philosophy. Yet in the final analysis, his work is of such a nature that it "yields its secrets," as Cocteau would say, only under this kind of scrutiny. In the first place, it is an art whose importance lies not in its content or in the *signifié* (which is the domain of traditional criticism) but, rather, in its structures, in its *signifiants,* and in the relationships they imply. Second, Cocteau's art does not "mean"; instead, it "evokes" because it manifests itself as a system of signs. To appreciate it fully, therefore, the public has to decipher its code and not satisfy itself with remaining a passive observer. Third, the work's significance resides not so much in its existence *qua* art (although it is certainly important in the history of twentieth-century art), but in its status as a reflection of a set of shared mental structures.

When I began my work on Cocteau, my goal was simply to solve the problem of coherence within the opus as a whole. Instead of attempting to impose a false unity by unsuitable methods of analysis, I tried to identify recurring elements—whatever they happened to be—which constituted an underlying system. As I had suspected, no real continuity existed insofar as content was concerned, but on the level of forms, structures and techniques, a well-defined esthetic unity emerged. Cocteau's view of art was apparently what unified his production, because the relationship among elements of the esthetic triad (artist, art-object, public) as well as the function of each element remained constant throughout everything he created. As I examined the esthetic system uncovered, however, I realized that Cocteau's esthetic stance had not come into existence *ex nihilo*. As soon as I raised the question of why his art took the forms it did (what sort of perceptual mode had produced such an art), I understood that his esthetic resulted directly from and stood as a response to his view of reality. The only access to his world-view lay in analysis of the structures and images (as opposed to the content) which served as bases for his critical essays as well as for his art. After having deduced the rather intricate system that constitutes his view of the world, having reviewed the intellectual and personal influences that shaped his life, and having placed these data in historical perspective (within the context of the 1970–1960 period), I concluded that in addition to being an artistic force in its own right, Cocteau's art mirrored the mental set and the existential dilemma common to an important segment of his generation. Most members of the group in the context of which Cocteau's work becomes revealing were upper-middle class; they probably could not have thought what they did (nor would they have been interested in thinking what they did) if they had not belonged to this class. However, their concerns resulted not solely from social position, but also from their moment in intellectual history. Since Cocteau is generally considered to be a frivolous artist, it has sometimes perplexed critics that the person to whom he most frequently alludes in his writings is Friedrich Nietzsche. Yet very few critics would dispute Nietzsche's intellectual dominance over many other artists who lived during the same period. An examination of Cocteau's work reveals that rather than an "aberration," Jean Cocteau was both a product—in the most passive sense—and a mirror of his time. As surely as with Gide, Montherlant, Sartre, or Malraux, the quandary that lay at the root of his art (and by the same token, at the root of his existential stance) was Nietzsche's "God is dead" and all that implies. Through his structures and his images, Cocteau was responding to the same kinds of questions as Sartre with his philosophical arguments. Each in his own way was reacting to a world in which a god who a priori bestows essence and external meaning on things does not exist; in which, then, nothing is given once and for all. Consequently, the *signifiant* and the *signifié* are split, and the individual perceiving consciousness becomes the only source of value and significance. From this point of view, power resides in being able to control the perception of other consciousnesses, since it is only through them—through the "Other"—that anyone or anything can be perpetuated in history. It is these struggles with nothingness, the Other, and history, which dominate Cocteau's art.

The principal factor that obscures Cocteau's affinity with his contemporaries is the intuitive, non-reasoned nature of his production: the work as a whole appears ambiguous primarily because it does not emanate from an analytic relationship with the world or with art. Proust, Malraux, Gide, Montherlant, Anouilh, Maeterlinck or Apollinaire, for example, have no claim to being philosophers in a systematic sense, but their work nevertheless must be situated within a framework where ideas and arguments are important. Whether he wrote novels, plays, or verse, each of these artists took words and concepts seriously. Mallarmé, Jarry, and Lautréamont in their different ways often claimed not to do so, but all three (with the obvious exception of Jarry at certain periods of his life) appear to have had intellectual control over what they created. Rimbaud began his journey toward a *dérèglement des sens* consciously. Even Breton, whose esthetic position was deliberately antilogical, wrote the highly articulate *Manifestes du*

surréalisme. What distinguishes Cocteau from many
artists of his generation (indeed, from much of
French art) is the lack of a stable conceptual base
directing his creations. Therefore, while his works frequently appear superficial, the principles that gener-
ated them and their coherence as a unit remain
difficult to grasp.

Many painters claim that for them the act of
creation must take place almost without thought: if
they stopped to analyze or to intellectualize what
they were doing, their creativity would somehow be
inhibited and ultimately destroyed. Some of them
also claim that they express themselves visually because they cannot communicate effectively with
words: their medium must be one of color and images.
Ironically—for he has the reputation of being a verbal
master—Cocteau actually seems to have shared many
more esthetic tendencies with *artistes graphiques* than
with writers. The entire range of his work—and this
includes novels, plays, poetry, film and *art graphique*—exists not primarily as a vehicle for concepts or
arguments about the nature of the real, but as an intuitive evocation of reality's structures. When Cocteau used language, it was frequently connotative
rather than denotative. Its power resided in sounds
and images, in puzzles and teases, in ambiguity and
indirectness. Instead of depending on logic or on an
overt attempt to come to terms with the human condition, its appeal lay in associations and allusions.
Cocteau himself even in his theoretical writings (for
they, too, are for the most part dependent upon
images) never specified what directed his work, and
since his opus is so varied, and many of his creations

are "occasional" or dated, the very nature of his work
tends to obscure the complex forces that produced it.

What I intend to argue in the following pages is,
first, that the diversity of Cocteau's opus as a whole
and the apparent accessibility of individual pieces
mask a consistent, elaborate world-view. However,
because Cocteau does not seem to have reacted to or
attempted to act upon existence analytically, he
never formulated his "position," and, as many visual
artists, he probably would have been incapable of
doing so. Hence, in order to uncover his premises,
the critic must deduce them from his work; not from
the words themselves (since they are seldom used
literally) but from the patterns, structures, and forms
that recur. The two foci around which everything else
revolves are his intuition that reality is illusory and
unstable and his frequently stated belief that all
processes follow a pre-determined, ineluctable course.
(The ubiquitous figure of the double; a fascination
with games, codes, and deception; a highly fluid use
of language; and the multi-layered composition of his
works—all point to a fragmented real that is becoming
rather than being, a real that has no essence in the
metaphysical sense of the word. For Cocteau phenomena, if these are to be understood, cannot merely
be perceived. They must be interpreted rather than
accepted, for the universe is structured as a *boîte-
à-malices*, a machine that by definition tricks and
deceives.)

Second, Cocteau's art served the same purpose as
did his drugs: it represented an attempt to overcome
fragmentation. Rather than growing solely out of fi-
nancial or social pressures as his critics frequently

claim, his esthetic (defined as his conception of the
artist/art-object/public triad) resulted directly from
his perception of the world. He needed the act of
creation as a weapon, as protection, as an instrument
of power. Since his relationship to his work seems to
have been highly emotional, his art reflected rather
than intellectualized an existential stance, and the
role of creation for him remained highly personal: he
was not an artist for moral or social reasons. His art
existed primarily for him, for his ego, for his salvation, rather than for some ultimate betterment of the
human condition. He intended his works to be spectacular and effective for him and his time, for his own
audience; he did worry about his reputation with
posterity, but the present was of obvious concern.

Within the context of his world view, art appears to
have had a double role. First, as *spectacle* (regardless
of genre) or entertainment, it provided a release from
solitude and nihilism. That a spectator might be able
to enjoy a work on a purely emotional plane and to
lose himself as a child would in an atmosphere
féerique et merveilleux remained one of Cocteau's
major goals throughout his career. On this level art
functioned as a means of *divertissement*. On a second
level, however, it became a means of forming or
directing reality itself: the artist resembled a child
guarded by a star, a child who could manipulate the
real with his games. In this context Cocteau's intricate mythology clearly illustrates the interdependence between his life and his creation. The child-
creator (or the "angel") emerged as hero in the motifs
of the fall and of redemption which form his work's
basic pattern. Incarnating what Cocteau called "great

disorders"—incest, homosexuality, parricide—the artist himself was necessarily destroyed but his work retained the potential of vindicating ultimately everything he has represented: if he is lucky, in the course of time the public may come to admire characters like Oedipus who were once cast out because they represented disorder but who have become heroes through ritual and legend—through the work of art. Only the artist, it seems, has a chance of controlling perception, hence reality. Only he as a child remaining close to primeval forces can influence or shape an unstable real in order to create some semblance of harmony and unity. His are the only games that can challenge nature's. For Cocteau, then, art fulfilled the same function in life as rites and incantation did for primitive man: it resembled a kind of game, but a vital one that became real, that shielded its participants from existence as it gave them power (however unsubstantial or imaginary the power may appear) over it.

Among the genres with which Cocteau experimented, theater epitomized what he sought in art. The nature of dramatic experience (spectacle, ritual, game-playing) constituted a synthesis of all the forms he utilized during his career. Ultimately, such of his novels as *Thomas l'Imposteur* or *Les Enfants Terribles* depicted games so successful that they triumphed over reality; they imply a kind of ultimate theater. For him, poetry reading (poetry never lacked an aural dimension for Cocteau) participated in spectacle. His graphic work seems to have evolved from other genres and to have given them a visual dimension. In theater he brought together the play eulogized in his novels,

the verbal power and tricks underlying his poetry,
and the craft involved in his *art graphique*. His contact with the stage began in his childhood and lasted
until his death. Theater, then, stands as the crossroads
of his talents and the unity of his esthetic.

An obvious question arises insofar as cinema is
concerned. Although Cocteau's films can illuminate
details of his thought, it would be an error to view
them as central to the development of his world view,
his mythology, or his esthetic. First of all, with the
exception of *Le Sang d'un Poète* (1930), they appeared relatively late in his career; they are derivative
in that they depend on the images, motifs, and values
already present in preceding novels, verse, and plays.
In fact, the associations upon which Cocteau built
remain unclear outside the context of the whole
opus. The angel, the poet, Annamese and Chinese
characters, Dargelos, the artist's fate, and mirrors, to
give just a few examples from *Le Sang d'un Poète*, are
all clearly threads drawn from earlier creations.
Rather than indicating new paths in the evolution of
a mental set, cinema provided a new tool of expression, an opening of technical horizons. Cocteau said,
for instance, that with the camera's help he could
place each spectator in a privileged position with the
actors; he could easily manipulate time and dream
sequences; he could reach greater numbers of people.
Second, instead of a totally independent art form, his
film esthetic represents a broadening of theater's
power. Frequently, the same actors and decorators
staffed both drama and film, and much of Cocteau's
cinematic production grew out of adaptations or
direct transpositions of his plays. Moreover, his

theoretical statements about film are in many cases
identical to the goals he set for the stage. Hence, it
seems that in Cocteau's field of reference, all art
forms which combine visual and aural effects participate in a first order of creation, since they are not
limited to description: they show rather than discuss.
They all rely on seduction and ritual, on ceremonial
techniques that can liberate participants from a mundane existence. Finally, they have the capacity to
transform what Cocteau would call the artist's *phan-
tasmes* into reality. At different periods of his life,
Cocteau praised theater and film for the manner in
which they could be structured through complex
images, for the role attributed to signs rather than to
meaning, and for the potential each had to become a
kind of "total art." For these reasons, I believe that
in terms of esthetics and world view, theater and cinema belong in the same category but that Cocteau's
theater provides a much fuller, more complex insight
into his mind than his films do, although the latter
are useful in elucidating many problems.

During his lifetime Jean Cocteau came into contact
with and responded to many of the most far-reaching
artistic and intellectual currents of the last third of
the nineteenth century and of the first half of the
twentieth. He has frequently been characterized as a
sort of crossroads where ideas and artistic tendencies
met and where they were transformed into spectacle-
like creations. What has not been pointed out, however, is the extent to which Cocteau's mind reflects a
crossroads in history when an intellectual elite was
struggling to effect a transition between a world en-
dowed a priori with meaning and a world in which

values and meaning reside not in God but in each
human consciousness. In no sense could it be argued
that Cocteau was one of Nietzsche's "descendants"
in the conscious way Malraux was, for example. What
he illustrates is the emotion at the base of *The Birth
of Tragedy* as opposed to the intellectual force
behind the book, because he, perhaps more than any
other influential French artist of his time, responded
to the real affectively rather than analytically: he
seemed incapable of placing an intellectual distance
between himself and the world. In the final analysis,
what remains significant about his art is the portrait
of the structures of consciousness that lies hidden
within it and the kind of response this portrait reveals to a period of chaos and reevaluation. Other
artists very deliberately attempted to communicate a
message to their respective publics; they used art
primarily as a vehicle for their ideas because—to some
degree at least—they had come to intellectual terms
with their dilemma. They might be said to represent
progress toward Nietzsche's "superman." Less independent, less reflective, and certainly less sure of himself than they, Cocteau utilized his art as a personal
exorcism or as a protection against reality instead of as
an affirmation of knowledge: he appears to have been
incapable of moving beyond the status of a dependent
being. Because of this, he relied more heavily on spectacle than his contemporaries did, and consequently
he strongly influenced what theater was to become in
the 1950's. On the other hand he left the mirror-
image of a man whose response to nihilism, flux, and
uncertainty was that not of a conqueror but of a
victim.

1. Cocteau's Milieu

Although much of the confusion surrounding Jean Cocteau exists as a result of his personal life, it is impossible simply to ignore his world and associations or to relegate them to the level of trivia. The structure of his life represents a fitting introduction to the way he perceived the world, because the ambiguity that characterizes his work also permeated his existence. What one discovers is an amalgamation of camp and splendor, of cabaret sketches and plays presented at the Comédie Française, of official praise and insidious denigration. The same person who created *Les Mariés de la Tour Eiffel* and *Le Boef sur le toit* also produced *Le Jeune Homme et la mort* and *Les Parents terribles*. He managed to participate in a *boulevard* tradition as well as in homosexual, elite "in-group" creations. He was supposedly born into a comfortable, upper-middle class family, but he obviously lacked the money he frequently solicited from aristocratic patrons and other wealthy friends. Since Francis Steegmuller's excellent, detailed biography has already shed a great deal of light on Cocteau's life and period, I have simply indicated patterns which are significant for an understanding of his relationship with the world and with art.

Among the first adjectives brought to mind while
thinking about Jean Cocteau is surely the word
"Parisian" with all its connotations of sophistication
and of elegance. Aware of his roots or origins, he himself once remarked that he was born Parisian and that
he spoke Parisian. The fabric of his existence was in-
separable from his birthplace. Therefore, unlike
Anouilh who came to the capital from Bordeaux and
who supposedly retains the accent of his province, or
many foreign artists such as Picasso, Beckett, Ionesco,
and Gertrude Stein, he was distinctly urban and
French: at first glance, he appears to have none of the
difficulties of a man in exile or of a rebel.

In addition, Cocteau is to a great extent associated
with a social and artistic elite: born in Maisons-Lafitte,
a wealthy suburb, of a family deeply interested in the
arts, he formed an integral part of the complex network representing the creative avant-garde of his time,
and his is an experience that spans the first sixty
years of the century. He collaborated with innovators
in every domain; he brought together people and
ways of life that without him might never have come
into contact; he was a crossroads, a catalyzer. His
initial active participation in theater, for example,
was designing *affiches* or advertising posters for
Diaghilev's Ballets Russes, the company which was to
appear in *Parade,* his first work for the stage, a work
which has recently been revived by the Joffrey Ballet
Company. Picasso designed the curtain and masks for
Parade (which provoked a scandal when presented in
1917), Dufy the masks for *Le Boeuf sur le toit*, and
Coco Chanel the costumes of *Orphée* and of *Antigone*
(because, as Cocteau explained, he could not imagine

Oedipus' daughters badly dressed). Serge Lifar
choreographed *Phèdre*, and the present director of
the Casino de Paris, Roland Petit, a talented, experimental impresario in everything relating to the dance
(for example, his *Carmen* or his adaptation of *A la
Recherche du Temps Perdu* scheduled to celebrate
the centennial of the Opéra in 1975), was the choreographer of *Le Jeune Homme et la mort*.

Musicians are certainly not lacking in Cocteau's
circle of collaborators. A score by Erik Satie forms
the background of *Parade*. Stravinsky's grandiose
oratorio *Oedipus Rex* is based on a text of Cocteau
translated into Latin and some of its most successful
productions have been those in which the latter's
tableaux vivants with their symbolic masks render
visible the force and passion evoked by the music. In
terms of continuity, however, the Groupe des Six
(Francis Poulenc, Darius Milhaud, Arthur Honneger,
Georges Auric, Germaine Taillefer, and Louis
Durey) was probably Cocteau's most important
musical affiliation, since it remained strong throughout his career. United in a negative rather than a pos-
itive sense by a revolt against the vagueness of Debussy
or the classicism of Fauré and by its attempted break
with traditional composition in general, the Group
provided the point of departure of Cocteau's early
essay *Le Coq et l'Arlequin* in which he praised efforts
of young artists to incorporate the modern, popular
spirit of jazz and of the music hall into their work.
With the exception of Louis Durey, each member
contributed to the *merveilleux quotidien* that dominates *Les Mariés de la Tour Eiffel*. In 1920 Milhaud's
lively Brazilian melodies accompanied the dreamlike

movements of *Le Boeuf sur le toit*, and in 1927 his
whimsical folktunes formed the background of *Le
Pauvre Matelot*. Honegger orchestrated the dissonant
score that acts as a conterpoint to the voices in *Antigone*. Auric composed music for the ballet *Phèdre*.

Even if Cocteau's disparate vocations of novelist,
film-maker, poet, and painter are simply mentioned
in passing, then, his presence in artistic circles, as is
evident from his experiences in theater, can be described only as ubiquitous. Although he supposedly
was constantly at war with Breton, whose *coterie*
allegedly provoked the tumult at the opening night of
Parade, surrealist influences abound in *Le Boeuf sur
le toit, Les Mariés de la Tour Eiffel, Orphée*, and even
La Machine infernale: the importance of dreams and
of the subconscious, a juxtaposition of contradictory
faces of reality, persistent demythifications accomplished by an awareness of heretofore undiscovered
beauties in the everyday world, and inquiries into the
role of the poet and the nature of inspiration pervade
these plays. Likewise, it is impossible to deny the role
of Picasso and the cubist painters, of their attempt to
discern the basic elements of a whole and to recon-
struct it differently. Extrapolating from their visual
effects, from their work in collage and *trompe-l'oeil*,
Cocteau strove to utilize their discoveries in an audi-
tory form with his *trompe-l'oreille*, never success-
fully carried out, in *Parade*. At the source of such
experiments lay a post World War I sensibility—*l'esprit
nouveau ou moderne*—usually associated with Apollinaire and formulated by him in "L'Esprit nouveau
et les poètes," "Zone," "La Jolie Rousse," and *Les
Peintres cubistes*: a questioning of old values; both

perplexity and anticipation in the face of having to
adapt to the twentieth century's complexity; awareness of having witnessed the death of an epoch and of
a civilization through participation in a war which
resembled a *rite de passage*, a transition to a higher
level of consciousness; comprehension of the increas-
ing importance of the mechanical, of machines, of the
airplane; and, most important from the point of view
of esthetics, an inquiry into the kind of art suitable
for this new world, an art capable of reflecting the tele-
graph and ragtime as well as the fragmented nature of
a human being, the complex, frantic networks of
activity that make up a large city. In part, such are
the themes that reappear in *Parade, Le Coq et l'Arlequin*, "Les Ballets suédois et les jeunes," and many
other of Cocteau's writings concurrent with Apollinaire's theories or *Les Mamelles de Tiresias*. Hence,
from the beginning of his career Cocteau has been
viewed by some critics as a parasite, a dilettante, and
an imitator totally lacking in originality. After all, it
is argued, his association with the Ballets Russes and
Diaghilev's "Etonne-moi" are the sources of his concept of spectacle and the *raison d'être* of his first
attempts at creation for the stage. *Orphée* is merely a
homosexual farce inspired by his insincere conversion
to Catholicism and by his dabbling in surrealism.
L'Aigle à deux têtes suspiciously resembles *Ruy Blas*
of which he had made a film the year before; *Bacchus*
is a shadow of Sartre's *Le Diable et le bon dieu*.
Neither choreographer nor dancer nor musician, he is
but the *animateur* of the ballets associated with his
name and which, like much of his drama, are restate-
ments of well-known archetypes. Similar evaluations

mark his involvement in any artistic endeavor: his painting and drawing are slavish copies of Picasso, *Le Sang d'un poète* owes everythings to *Le Chien andalou*, *Thomas L'Imposteur* is the novel written in conjunction with Radiguet's *Le Bal du Comte d'Ogel*. For many, therefore, he is a dazzling figure who knew the geniuses of his time and who made use of their originality for his own minor talent: he remains the narrator of Stravinsky's *L'Histoire du soldat*, the voice in *La Machine infernale*, a participant in the Cannes film festival, the creator of familiar sketches of a star and of an angel.

Cocteau's world, however, is not one that can be understood only in terms of revolutionary and many times impecunious artists, of theories or experiments that changed the course of art in the twentieth century. As a glance at his life indicates, Cocteau was a part of a social circle that can best be described as *snob et mondain.* Not a man of great personal wealth, he was much of the time dependent upon protectors or sponsors. In fact, his first creative attempts as a young man appear to be those of a pampered salon poet. The Count Etienne de Beaumont, at whose lavish costume balls he was a frequent guest, commissioned the unusual ballet *Roméo et Juliette* for an elaborate group of spectacles, the Soirées de Paris, and provided funds necessary for *Le Boeuf sur le toit*. Princess Edmonde de Polignac financed his production of *Oedipus Rex*. For over ten years, he and his future executor Edward Dermit were the guests of Madame Francine Weisweiller at her villa Santo Sospir in Saint-Jean-Cap-Ferrat. *Le Train bleu*, one of his early ballets in collaboration with Diaghilev, was

inspired by the famous Blue Train that high society
took from Paris to the beach at Deauville. In addition,
his childhood memories of theater were those of the
monstre sacré tradition, of popular, influential actors
such as Sarah Bernhardt and Edouard de Max for
whose particular talents or personality plays were
conceived and who, idolized by the audience, became
more important than the role they were interpreting.
Cocteau associated himself with de Max's exotically
dressed, predominantly transvestite and homosexual
group of friends (the great actor arranged his first
public poetry reading) and later adopted in modified
form the practice of writing with a specific actor in
mind: he is responsible for the fame of Jean Marais,
for example. The acting tour de force *L'Aigle à deux
têtes* starred Marais and Edwige Feuillère; *Les Parents
terribles* was intended for Marais, Yvonne de Bray,
and Gabrielle Dorziat. Each of these artists was a
favorite of the sophisticated theater-going public,
each *première* was a social event for the Tout Paris.
Associated with Cocteau's name, therefore, are the
theaters and night clubs of the Champs Elysées, the
wealth of the eighth and sixteenth arrondissements,
the glamor of the aristocracy or of the *haute bourgeoisie*. The question has often arisen as to the influence of such a milieu on his art. It is often claimed
that for monetary reasons he capitulated to the taste
of his protectors or of his audience, that in many instances he created only to entertain a superficial,
blasé public: hence, one reason for the derogatory
connotations of the term *texte-pré-texte*, a script that
has no purpose other than that of being transformed
into *spectacle*, whether its ultimate goal be to provide

a virtuoso part for an actor (*L'Aigle à deux têtes, La Voix humaine*), to fill the stage with harmonized light, movement, and sound (*Roméo et Juliette*), or to create a mood through incantation (*Renaud et Armide*).

The final aspect of Cocteau's "visibility" (a word he used to denote his public image) which pertains to his theater is his fascination with what might be termed the "minor" arts: the circus, nightclubs, music halls, jazz. Much of the *théâtre de poche*—for example, *Le Bel Indifférent*—consists of sketches evidently inspired by and at times destined for nightclub performances of a single actor. Written for Edith Piaf, who performed it first at the Théâtre des Bouffes Parisiens and later at the more sophisticated Théâtre Marigny and at the Théâtre du Palais-Royal, it is based on the traditional, somewhat sordid duo of overwrought woman and her unfaithful, unconcerned gigolo. With its detached male character and its frantic, garrulous heroine, *Lis ton journal* is in the same vein. However, the subject matter of this little collection is as varied as its ultimate goal is set. "Le Menteur" is a long, difficult solo that develops Cocteau's self-description, "Je suis un mensonge qui dit toujours la vérité," and highlights the thread of mythomania recurring throughout his work. On the other hand, "Je l'ai perdue" derives much of its semi-comic effect from the sexual orientation of the plot. Presented as a plea before a judge and constructed around a transvestite *quiproquo* in which an older man falls in love with a youth who has disguised himself as a girl in an effort to avoid the police, the scene inevitably culminates in a discovery of the "young lady's" true sex. The

virtuoso monologues that Cocteau often employed
in his "serious" drama are frequently reminiscent
of the *théâtre de poche* and imply a faith in the
power of the actor to lure or even to hypnotize his
public. Roles such as that of the Sphinx (usually
associated with Lucienne Bogaert) in *La Machine
infernale,* of the abandoned woman (Berthe Bovy)
in *La Voix humaine* or of the enchantress Armide
in *Renaud et Armide* probably have their origin in the
playwright's collaboration in songs and soliloquies
where an individual talent becomes all-important.
Arletty and Marianne Oswald are well-known per-
formers for whom he composed, but the epitome of
the genre is certainly to be found in the interpretations of Piaf: toward the end of her life when her
ravaged face made her look much older than she was
and when her health was failing, she nevertheless
transcended her physical self as soon as her voice
filled a hall and enmeshed the listeners.

Although the influence on Cocteau of Negro
bands and of the circus (the leading roles of *Le
Boeuf sur le toit* went to the Fratellini Brothers) is
undeniable, it was never so strong or so enduring as
that of cafe society, of *boîtes de nuit,* of the *demi-
monde,* or of female impersonators. What unifies
the *théâtre de poche* and permeates much of his
theater as a whole is a sense of intimacy between
performer and audience, a feeling of the "in group,"
of a private world that characterizes certain cabarets
or nightclubs. The very success of "Je l'ai perdue"
with its combination of the burlesque and the sca-
brous or of "Le Bel indifférent" depends on a
sophisticated, mature audience familiar with the

milieu of the gigolo or of the kept woman, of the
homosexual or of the transvestite.

Since in any such art a definite knowledge and participation on the part of the spectator are assumed (if
the audience lacks the requisite social background per-
mitting it to appreciate connotations or allusions,
the thrust of the work remains incomplete), Cocteau's
collaboration in nightclub entertainment reflects (or,
perhaps, prefigures) the sensitivity to myth that distinguishes whatever he creates. Though it is evident
that theater as a whole depends on a recognition of
signs by the public, Cocteau intentionally drew full advantage from archetypal and stock situations. An entire popular tradition emerges from his sketches:
badly furnished hotel rooms, unhappy lovers, an oblivious man behind his newspaper.

In-group aspects of these performances however are
not merely a result of their music hall overtones.
More than any other feature of his theater, the atmosphere of his occasional pieces captures the essence of
an existence at the edge of society. In this context it
is pertinent to note the difference between *La Voix
humaine* and *Le Bel indifférent*. Whereas the former,
presented at the state-supported Comédie Française, is
almost bourgeois with its commonplace framework of
the mistress rejected by her lover who has decided to
marry another woman, the latter, cast in the same
basic pattern but intended for a different kind of
audience, is much harsher, devoid of most romantic
pretense: in the place of an impending marriage, only
the man's indifference separates the two people in
their hotel room, and nothing indicates that the woman's love was ever reciprocated.

"Je l'ai perdue" is directed at an even more restricted public. The narrator's explanation of her
boy friend's female dress—the latter's enjoyment of
his role, his "protector" who thinks him a virginal
young girl, and the fall down the stairs that puts an
end to the disguise—places the act in a *tradition
grivoise* to be sure, but the tone and details are
probably most fully appreciated by a worldly, largely homosexual group of spectators. Analagous,
somewhat personal associations that highlight a certain exclusiveness are often present in a more subtle
fashion in Cocteau's theater proper: the misogyny
frequently commented upon in *Orphée;* Jocasta's
personality in the first three acts of *La Machine infernale;* and, to a certain extent, her suicide by use of
a scarf, recalling Isadora Duncan's death. Hence, although his world is in general that of the Tout Paris,
Cocteau is more particularly affiliated with a segment of it where wealth and liberation from social
or moral norms merge: opium, boy friends, Edith
Piaf and her young husband Theo—all are basic
components of what Cocteau represents, facets as
essential to his being as his elegant speech or his
delicate hands.

If his reputation as a great synthesizer is many
times a derogatory label, it is nevertheless impres-
sive, if only because of the diversity it implies. Few
men have participated in such heterogeneous activities or known so many people from disparate walks
of life. Cocteau was a member of the French and
Belgian academies as well as a recipient of an honor-
ary doctorate from Oxford University. According to
Simone de Beauvoir, it was he who introduced Jean

Genet to Sartre. Through his newspaper articles, he was
partially responsible for the 1938 comeback of Al
Brown, whom he called a poet of boxing. Yet, as Steegmuller has pointed out, though he was instrumental in
introducing artists of Montparnasse to Right Bank
society, Cocteau himself, in spite of his numerous
acquaintances, should not be associated primarily with
the Left Bank. Of the theaters where premieres of his
plays were held, not one is located there, and the three
groups into which most of the playhouses fall are a
telling summary of his activity. There are, of course,
state theaters such as the Opéra *(Phèdre, Le Jeune
Homme et la mort)* and the Comédie Française *(La
Voix humaine, Renaud et Armide)* which reflect his
status as an acknowledged representative of French
letters; *salles* along the Champs-Elysées (Théâtre des
Ambassadeurs, Théâtre Marigny, Théâtre des Champs-
Elysées); numerous experimental or popular theaters
scattered from the second arrondissement to the
Pigalle area and westward to the Boulevard des Ba-
tignoles (Théâtre des Arts, Nouveau Théâtre Antoine,
Théâtre de l'Atelier and de l'Oeuvre, Théâtre Hébertôt, and the Bouffes Parisiens). Although the influence
of the Montparnasse cubists, especially Picasso, on
Cocteau is undeniable, their importance in his theater
is restricted to his earliest productions. Court Etienne
de Beaumont and his circle based in the seventh arrondissement aside, Cocteau's Bohemia appears to be
concentrated around the region of Montmartre. Moreover, if the term "Left Bank" is taken to mean the
intellectual centers of university students or of Sartre
(the Latin Quarter and Saint-Germain des Prés) this is
not at all his milieu: he never wrote for the more radi-

cal little playhouses like the Théâtre de la Huchette
or the Mouffetard, for example, and his audience is
not that of Genet, Beckett, or the Ionesco of *Les
Chaises*. Moreover, he has never been a part of an intellectual left, and it would be impossible to describe
him as an *éscrivain engagé* in any political or social
sense. Unlike Sartre, Camus, or—to choose a contemporary playwright—Arrabal, he had little interest in
questions of poverty or revolution, of morality and
right. Unlike Beckett or Ionesco, he did not overtly
dramatize metaphysical thought or anguish in the face
of the human condition: his was not an intellectual
theater, it was not primarily a vehicle for ideas.
Rather, his obvious respect for virtuosity coupled
with his fusion of painting, music, and dance into a
single dramatic experience implied a spectacle-oriented
conception of art.

Coming to terms with Cocteau would be simple if
he were only his "visible" self: he could be dismissed
as a brilliant but empty phenomenon of twentieth-
century art, an ageless child who never tired of playing
games. Behind the complex yet accessible network of
his public life, however, lie elements that identify him
with the universe of Colette or Proust, with a private
world and a closed room. No aspect of his existence
commonly alleged as proof of his creative limitations
can be placed into a neat category that necessarily
implies a certain type of art. His experiments with
drugs, whatever their origin and however faddish they
may seem, led to cures, some paid for by Chanel,
and, afterward, according to *Opium,* to a state resembling abulia: everything appeared totally gratuitous, without meaning. His numerous boy friends—

Jean Marais, Raymond Radiguet, Maurice Sachs, and
Jean Desbordes are among the best known—culminated
in his legal adoption of Edward Dermit, perhaps his
most public manifestation of desire for a son. His associations with elegant society, with protectors, are not
just masquerades of grace and sycophancy: shortly before his death, he broke with Mme Weisweiller, and his
journal *Le Passé défini* cannot yet be released by Gallimard because of its potentially libelous content. If one
wants to relate Cocteau to a social or psychological
context, the bitterness, disappointment, and divisions
in his life must be remembered, since they are in part
the outgrowth of a decadent, wealthy stratum that
was as cruel as it was beautiful: the Guermantes'
deep egocentrism, Charlus' male brothel and his maso-
chism, and Chéri's nihilistic indifference are faithful
depictions of its reality.

2. The Nature of the Real

1. Jean Cocteau, *Le Cordon ombilical* (Paris: Plon, 1962), p. 15.

The divisions and contradictions apparent in Cocteau's life manifest themselves as persistent facets of his work: at first glance, on the level of content, the opus taken as a whole appears to lack unity, and relationships among individual elements seem tenuous. Yet on the levels of structure, form, and archetypes, a definite coherence emerges that reflects a consistent stance in regard to the world and that sketches what Cocteau would call his "self-portrait":

En vérité, les personnages qui peuplent notre oeuvre ont moins d'importance que son architecture. Attacher de l'importance à l'anecdote revient à juger un peintre d'après ses modèles au lieu de découvrir son auto-portrait dans la manière de les peindre.[1]

If one were to attempt to identify a core of terms that described his art and implied the nature of his world view, it would of necessity include such words as "cipher," "hieroglyph," "code," "game," "trick," "mystery," "ceremony," "mask," and "symbol." In many ways each work exists as a closed logical system, deceptively constructed so that the premises and their implications are not immediately obvious. Fre-

quently, moreover, the puzzle has a double order: just
as the public finds itself bewildered by aspects of the
art-object, characters in the works lack knowledge of
crucial aspects of their reality, hence cannot interpret
it properly. On both levels, what is perceived appears
to be constructed of taunting signs linked by ricochets.
In Cocteau's universe, then, phenomena are by definition double-edged and therefore must be interpreted
rather than accepted: the code has to be broken if
either the world or the work of art is to be understood.
On every level (conception, text, presentation), the
form unifying Cocteau's work is that of the double
(of the transvestite, for example), of illusion, of a
reality that must be deciphered. Turning specifically
to Cocteau's theater (although the following analyses
are applicable to each genre in which he worked), we
can determine that plot, structure, and dramatic techniques all reflect this basic existential stance.

Few Cocteau characters have more than a partial
understanding of their universe: at every turn, they
perceive but a fraction of what is significant. Frequently, the very core or generating principle of a play can
be described only as a search, a riddle, or a problem to
be solved. Since it is a detective story in which one
of the major characters must discover the identity of
an anonymous letter writer, *La Machine à écrire*
comes to mind as the most evident example of such
a framework. Obviously, in *La Machine infernale*,
Oedipus begins his journey toward destruction by
attempting to grapple with the enigma of his birth,
and consequently by answering the Sphinx's question. The crux of the tragedy resides in his being destined to misinterpret essential signs, in his inability to

decipher correctly. Orpheus receives "poetic" and incomprehensible messages from an unusual horse, and
the phrase "Madame Eurydice reviendra des enfers"
baffles him because he does not know how to read it.
At the end of the first act of *Les Chevaliers de la
Table Ronde*, Arthur's men set out on a comic, disor-
ganized quest for the Grail as their bewildered king
tries to come to terms with the mysterious events at
court. On a more abstract level, *L'Aigle à deux têtes*,
Renaud et Armide, and in a completely different
fashion, *Le Jeune Homme et la mort* represent attempts to resolve difficulties in love, difficulties that
often arise from failures to understand each other's
language.

Were the Coctelian universe a simple one, there
would be few dilemmas arising from the interpretation of signs. In Cocteau's theater, however, reality
manifests itself as a coexistence of many levels that
are often contradictory and frequently have very
little in common. Yet these levels mesh so tightly as
to appear indistinguishable. Hence, an intricate, both-
and type of juxtaposition characterizes a world that
simultaneously includes opposites: the banal and the
poetic, the pedestrian and the marvelous, the serious
and the farcical all mingle to form a complex, deceptive network where each element has equal value. The
nature of the real, as it can be deduced from Cocteau's works, is elusive, then, because it is composite
("double" at the very least): the structure of each
play represents an amalgam of the commonplace with
magic or the supernatural (*Orphée, La Machine infernale, Les Chevaliers de la Table Ronde, Renaud et
Armide, Les Mariés de la Tour Eiffel*); with games

(*L'Aigle à deux têtes, Les Monstres sacrés, Les Cheva-liers de la Table Ronde, Bacchus*); with dreams (*Les Chevaliers, La Machine infernale*); or with different sorts of time (*Orphée, Renaud et Armide, Les Chevaliers*).

   It is difficult to imagine a more composite play than *Orphée*. Described by Cocteau himself as "moitié farce, moitié méditation sur la mort,"[2] the work evolved from a one-act play about the birth of Jesus in which an angel was disguised as one of Joseph's carpenter aides.[3] Suspicious of the birth, the towns-people chased the family away. Thus vestiges of the work's source remain in its final form. Mary and Joseph become Eurydice and Orpheus, who is a poet; Heurtebise, without their knowing it, is a guardian angel; poetry takes the place of a baby, and the Bacchantes resemble the villagers who did not recog-nize the important event coming to pass in their midst; the final ascent of Orpheus, Eurydice, and Heurtebise may be a reflection of some original reference to salvation after death. Juxtaposed with "sacred" elements, the magical and the everyday in-tertwine to create a baffling, often burlesque, whole. In addition to two levels of myth—Christian and Greek—the spectator finds himself before a *ménage à trois* situation in which one member is a horse from whom Orpheus receives poetic inspiration through cryptic messages. Side by side with the inexplicable horse (who has human legs) and the poet's comically reverent attitude toward him, some of Cocteau's most cherished beliefs about poetry form one of the play's theoretical aspects: striving for a transforma-tion of poetry, the artist must plunge into his own

2. Jean Cocteau, and André Fraig-neau, *Entretiens avec André Fraig-neau* (Paris: Union général des éditions, 1965), p. 51.
3. Ibid., p. 53.

4. Cocteau,
Théâtre I (Paris:
Grasset, 1957),
pp. 129-130.

subconscious and discover the unknown; he must scandalize those around him with his works, because scandal clears the air. Heurtebise the angel disguised as a glazier comforts Eurydice the unhappy wife, teaches Orpheus how to pass unscathed from life to Death, and disappears while talking to a pretentious police commissioner who evidently takes no stock in magic. Therefore, as Orpheus realizes, he is living in the midst of forces that surpass him and that he cannot understand:

> Orphee. . . . *Que savons-nous? Qui parle? Nous nous cognons dans le noir; nous sommes dans le surnaturel jusqu'au cou. Nous jouons à cache-cache avec les dieux. Nous ne savons rien, rien, rien.*[4]

Hence, with the commonplace and the supernatural as its poles, *Orphée* encompasses a whole series of opposing states of reality.

Moreover, a great variety of dramatic resources underscores the complexity of the play's structure. In addition to drawing on obvious tragic, comic, and *boulevard* elements, Cocteau attacked the *pièce bien faite* on the levels of convention and structure. At the end of the play, for example, after the women of the city—Maenads in contemporary form—pursued Orpheus and tore off his head ("dismembered" him), Heurtebise (creating a kind of spoof on the idea of a poet immortalized by a bust) placed the head on a pedestal in order that it not be noticed: after all, it would look "natural" there. Since the angel could not think of a name or address at the request of the policeman investigating the poet's death, the actor portraying Orpheus substituted his own voice and, like a *deux ex machina*, supplied the necessary information through the mouth of the head. Moreover, he identified himself as "Jean Cocteau" and used Cocteau's own address. Therefore, the resolution of *Orphée* depends on totally unorthodox techniques, on a blatantly evident, defiant, *truquage*. Dramatic illusion is destroyed as a spectator contributes his watch while Orphée travels through Hell, and layers of reality are jumbled to an even greater degree than that depicted in the work itself: the stage, life, magic, death—none exhibits clear boundaries. All facets of the real coexist with indistinguishable value. *Orpheus*, whatever it may seem at first, is a highly experimental play insofar as dramatic techniques are concerned. Drawing from all types of theater, Cocteau created a work of heterogeneous spirit, both light and somber.

In *Les Chevaliers de la Table Ronde* and *La Machine infernale*, as in *Orphée*, a great diversity of tone or genre highlighted an intermingling of the supernatural and the commonplace. During the first two acts of *Les Chevaliers*, Arthur's castle lies under a spell cast by the sorcerer Merlin in order that Lancelot and Guenièvre may continue their adulterous affair unnoticed. All traditional order has vanished: seasons are no longer distinct, the sun never shines, and, as Merlin himself admits, debauchery and disorder reign. Their primary source is a fairly disreputable, obviously incompetent genie named Ginifer. Rescued by the sorcerer who needed him for his plans, Ginifer insists on calling his master "boss." Moreover, he expresses himself with an unmistakable lisp: all words like *"extraordinaire"* and *"exprès"* are pronounced

"*estraordinaire*" or "*esprès*" unless he thinks very
carefully about what he is saying. Ginifer's "talent"
supposedly lies in his ability to assume human form
and to imitate personalities. Unfortunately, his own
character traits are so distinctive that no matter
which body he happens to inhabit at a given time, no
matter how dignified the model may be, the behavior
pattern that emerges can be no other than Ginifer's.
For example, unknown to Arthur, Merlin spirited a-
way the "real" Gauvain and replaced him with his
hireling. Aware neither that his wife is unfaithful nor
that the children he accepts as his own are Lancelot's,
unhappy with his responsibilities as ruler and father,
with the serious attitude of his court, Arthur gladly
accepts the "change" in his nephew: he wants to
follow "Gauvain" to the servants' quarters and to the
kennels (after all, the people with whom Ginifer feels
the most comfortable are the *valets de chien*), he
enjoys watching his "nephew" attend court functions
indecently dressed in short pants. When Ginifer
attempts to imitate Guenièvre in the second act,
however, the effect can no longer remain one of mere
comedy: parody, slapstick, farce, and transvestite
humor make this scene between Lancelot and the little
genie one of the funniest in all of Cocteau's theater.
Throughout the play, Guenièvre appears as a discreet,
sensitive woman deeply in love with the knight and
worried about losing his affection. When "she" seeks
him out in Clingsor's castle, in contrast, "her" speech
is almost a parody of royal expression and "she"
cruelly emphasizes the illicit nature of their relationship:

La Fausse Reine. *Ouais, chevalier, perdez-vous le*
    sens? J'arrive dans cette chambre après avoir
    chevauché ventre à terre. Je monte les escaliers
    quatre à quatre et je trouve un juge. Pauvre neveu!
    Et moi qui le croyais remonté dans votre estime!
    Permettez-moi de trouver extraordinaire (elle sou-
    ligne l'x) *votre façon de recevoir votre reine et*
    votre maîtresse. Puis-je m'asseoir?
      Elle tombe assise dans le fauteuil.[5]

Having exclaimed that even adultery loses its charm
after eighteen years, "she" pretends—in a speech
comically reminiscent of *Phèdre*—to be madly in love
with someone else:

La Fausse Reine. *Bas les pattes. Il n'existe pas de*
    pacte entre nous, que je sache. Tout n'est pas
    éternel! J'aime Lancelot et j'aime (Elle boit en
    clignant de l'oeil) *J'aime . . . j'aime . . .*
Lancelot. *Galaad!*
La Fausse Reine. *C'est toi qui l'as nommé.*[6]

The more Ginifer drinks, the less he resembles the
Queen and the more outrageous his erotic ramblings
become, as he explains that King Ibert castrated
Clingsor in the very chateau where he and Lancelot
are talking (he had actually started to say "on lui a
coupé les couilles") and as he describes peeking
through the keyhole to catch a glimpse of Galaad
nude.

    Ginifer is, however, only the most obvious or non-
subtle manifestation of the supernatural in *Les*

7. Ibid., p. 235.   *Chevaliers.* In addition to the trials of Galaad "le très pur" and Lancelot's association with the spirits of the lake, which belong to the original *matière de Bretagne,* Merlin's magic flower, chalk circle, and ritualistic chants—as well as a haunted castle where doors open by themselves and invisible knights play chess—evoke a world not governed by ordinary laws.

Yet the play can hardly be characterized as a slapstick fairy tale. *Les Chevaliers* is at the same time farcical and tragic, *merveilleux* and *quotidien.* Lancelot and his children feel insecure and uncomfortable under Merlin's spell, although they do not understand exactly why their lives have changed: Lancelot believes that the reigning disorder is somehow his fault, that he is being punished. At the end of the play, when the sorcerer has lifted his *charme,* Arthur must face the reality of his wife's adultery, he must realize that Blandine and Segramor are not his children. All magic and play disappear as order and the ordinary return.

As has been noted, the action of *La Machine infernale* unfolds simultaneously on two planes: that of men and that of gods. The nature of reality is succinctly expressed by Anubis, the Sphinx's helper:

Anubis. *Obéissons. Le mystère a ses mystères.*
    Les dieux possèdent leurs dieux. Nous avons les
    nôtres. Ils ont les leurs. C'est ce qui s'appelle
    l'infini.[7]

The cosmos can be likened to a seemingly endless series of concentric spheres, each of which controls those contained within it. The various layers interact

for the most part without man's being aware that
something other than a known order is at work. Ap-
pearing against a stage set where peripheral darkness
evokes the realm of the gods, Anubis, Laius' ghost, the
Sphinx, and Tiresias represent the coexistence of the
supernatural with a *quotidien* that includes a complex
gamut of social strata and personality types. In the
first act, for example, the soldiers' slang, their attitude
toward authority, and their unperturbed acceptance of
a ghost reflect a mentality that recurs in the second act:
as the matron talks to the Sphinx, age-old preoccupations of common people (death in war, exploitation by
leaders) emerge. The historical moment has no importance, since the inhabitants of Thebes appear no different from Frenchmen who in 1934 felt threatened by the
chaotic economic and political situation. Jocasta, on the
other hand, in spite of the plague, obviously has no
material worries. In fact, she seems completely insensi-
tive to the city's problems. Portrayed at first as a silly,
scatterbrained, middle-aged woman interested only in
young men, she flirts with soldiers and shows no respect
for her priest. Oedipus acts like a stupid, pompous
braggart. His "victory" scene with the Sphinx is a parody, a demythification of all heroism.

The tension resulting from interaction between men
and the gods in *La Machine infernale* manifests itself
most clearly in the play's great variety of tones. Because
of characterizations (Jocasta, "Zizi," the soldiers), the
first act is slick in a fashion reminiscent of Boulevard
theater and cafe society, and Cocteau has been criticized for playing on such facile stereotypes as well as
for trying to be philosophical in the scene with the
Matron (Act Two). Although Jocasta's flirtations or

her attitude toward Tiresias are comic, Laius' futile
attempts to warn his wife of impending disaster and
evident foreshadowing devices (the brooch, the
scarf) create a mood almost diametrically opposed
to that of the frolicsome, slapstick scenes in *Les
Chevaliers:* at no time can the humor of *La Machine*
be described as other than cruel or mordant, since the
gods' games have little if anything to do with human
emotions. What dominates the first two acts behind
their comic or modern aspects is a derision that is
stripped of all humorous pretense in the monstrous
third act. Every detail (the stifling atmosphere of a
stormy night, the closed, blood-red wedding chamber,
Oedipus' and Jocasta's leaden movements, their nightmares, and intimacy that is painful for the audience
as well as for them) intensifies the image of systems
at war with one another, of taboos broken, of things
that should not be seen or done. Seventeen years after
the grotesque, distorted bedroom scene, Thebes, as at
the beginning of the play, has been placed under
seige, but in this case the noise from nightclubs and
the tinny, carnival setting have given way to a stark,
rapid *dénouement* resembling Sophocles' tragedy: the
human and the supernatural finally meet without
veils or masks.

   Renaud et Armide and *Les Mariés de la Tour Eiffel*
are the only two of Cocteau's plays in which no variety of genre or mood underscores the juxtaposition of
magic and the everyday. Written in alexandrines,
Renaud et Armide is a relentless tragedy that lacks
any mitigating gaiety. The play takes places in the un-
natural, metallic garden of Armide, who is an immortal, forever youthful enchantress. Renaud, who is king

of France, has somehow wandered into the garden and, bewitched, has fallen in love with the princess. Yet these two people remain eternally separated; they are from different realms. Since Armide belongs to a magic world, Renaud can never see her: not being human, she is unable to manifest herself in a human form—that is, in a form the king perceives as that of a woman. Even when she tries to make herself visible, she appears as a blinding, terrifying light, a kind of flame. Hence, during the duet in which the two declare their love for each other, they remain apart. Moreover, to love and be loved, Armide, who wears a ring that belonged to Orpheus, must sacrifice her immortality and leave the order of the fairies. By giving her ring to the man she chooses, she can make him love her, but his first kiss is destined to kill her. Therefore, if Renaud goes back to his homeland before kissing her, at his return he will find an older woman instead of the young girl he knew. If he kisses her before leaving, she will immediately die. Their dilemma has no resolution: Armide's nature, which prevents her from becoming human and links her eternally to her past, makes any sort of union impossible. Moreover, as Armide understood as soon as she removed her ring, Renaud's ties to his world are, like hers, eternal: he has a wife who will soon give birth to a child, his soldiers' drums recall his responsibilities as leader and conqueror. In *Renaud et Armide* irreconcilable systems—each with its own rules, each coherent in its own sphere—clash and destroy each other.

Just as *Renaud et Armide* has no relieving light, *Les Mariés* has no darkness; even more clearly than *Renaud et Armide*, *Les Mariés* is a work based on differences.

Both structurally and thematically, the play's development depends on the interaction of *le merveilleux*
with *le quotidien*. In his well-known 1922 preface
Cocteau analyzed the ambiguity of signs and the difficulties inherent in interpretation. The world portrayed
here—the world which occasioned Cocteau's ambition
to paint in a fashion he described as "truer than
true"—is definitely one of card tricks and sleights of
hand where strata of reality come into contact with
one another. For this reason almost every facet of the
Marié's construction is double. Instead of the action's
taking place directly, phonographs on either side of
the stage accompany it with a narration of events.
Rather than characters speaking to each other or
addressing the audience, the phonographs do all the
talking: they converse with each other as they comment on what they see, and they play out the characters' dialogues. *Le merveilleux* and *le quotidien*
form the structural spheres of the play, just as they
do, in another form, in *La Machine infernale*. As the
photographer explains at the beginning, in the place
of the little bird that traditionally flies out of a
camera, an ostrich flew out earlier in the day and the
machine hasn't worked properly since. Completely
oblivious to the situation, a staid, bourgeois wedding
party wanders through an apparently random series
of events centering on having its picture taken on the
Eiffel Tower. A bathing beauty and a lion climb out
of the camera and the photographer desperately pretends to be in complete control while the party continues to believe that everything is comprehensible
and as it should be. In a transposition of characteristics, the *appareil détraqué* seems to have a will of its

own but the human beings react mechanically and predictably. Likewise, Cocteau split action and dialogue of the play between actors and the phonographs, separating elements typically associated with each other and re-forming them in unusual ways, similar to the techniques Picasso often used. At every turn the supernatural so influences the world of every day that one can hardly describe reality as "simple" or "logical."

The supernatural is not the only element, however, that complicates any attempt at interpretation of the real in Cocteau's theater. For example, in addition to being a genie, Ginifer in *Les Chevaliers* plays games, and his impersonations, however clumsy they may seem, affect the perception of those around him. Though the role of play is minor in *Les Chevaliers*, in *Les Monstres sacrés, Bacchus,* and *L'Aigle à deux têtes* it becomes the major source of ambiguity, the master structure that puts the whole nature of reality into question.

Les Monstres sacrés is, most fittingly, a work about the theater. The principal character, Esther, is a great actress, a *monstre sacré* who believes that when she leaves the auditorium she leads a life completely divorced from the world of the stage. For her, at the beginning, acting represents "pretending" or make-believe: she makes a strong distinction between games or theater and the sincerity of life. One night when she is in her dressing room, a young actress, Liane, comes to her and claims that Florent, Esther's husband, who is also a popular actor, has asked her to marry him. At this moment, Esther's view of existence shifts radically; her simplicity and credulity in

8. Cocteau,
Théâtre II
(Paris: Grasset,
1957), p. 30.

regard to her marriage and ultimately in regard to life
in general appear to be no longer possible. She cannot
continue to live simply or unguardedly, to react spon-
taneously to the life she had accepted at face value.
An element of theater, of pretending, must thus ruin
the purity of her behavior, and she must begin to play
a role because Florent plays one, because he never
leaves the stage and lives naturally. Therefore, what
she had previously accepted as true, as completely
understood, proved to be illusory and, more important, dependent on interpretation. Her belief in a
stable core of reality can be seen only as a simplistic
view of the world.

   Although Esther soon discovers that the girl's dec-
laration was an attempt to play a starring role and
that her "confession" was a minutely planned scene,
what the older woman calls "le théâtre de la vie"[8]
has contaminated her unsuspecting outlook with
doubts. Liane's game might as well have been truth,
since it entered into a cause and effect relationship
with the force of a fact. Because of it Esther herself
must now construct a play to determine whether her
marriage had been merely an illusion of contentment.
The second act of *Les Monstres* is Esther's play: she
installs Liane in her home with Florent, takes the girl
as her student, and watches Liane's lie become reality.
Florent and Liane become lovers, Esther leaves home,
and Florent plans to marry his wife's pupil. It is in
this act that the confusion between reality and illusion, life and the theater becomes the most pronounced. Esther believes that she is not playing a role,
that she loves both Liane and Florent, that the three
are happy together. To Liane, however, Esther

appears as an actress who seems generous but who is
playing the part of generosity and self-sacrifice in
order to win her husband back. Liane believes that
for Esther and Florent the "arrangement," the
ménage à trois, represents "une vieille sentimentalité
de théâtre."[9] It appears, however, that although she
criticizes them for casting their lives as a play, she
hates Esther because the latter is upsetting her ideal
of herself as an actress and is challenging Liane's
desire to be the star-director who has the privilege of
arranging everything to suit her will. The entire act
is an endless mingling of the theater and of life to the
extent that it is impossible to distinguish truth from
fiction. An attitude which on the surface appears to
be a candid reaction may in fact be a cleverly arranged
trap. Games come to have exactly the same value as
reality.

In the third act, when Florent has tired of playing
his game with Liane and wants to return to the existence he had with Esther—that is, an existence in
which he can quit acting and live without the complications of a role—it is Esther who assumes a part. She
claims to be in love with someone else. For this
reason, Florent now sees his past no longer as boring
normality. Since he believes he has lost it, he views it
as an ideal and understands how Liane might have
been drawn to it as almost magically theatrical and
out of the ordinary.

At the end of the play Esther confesses that it is
Florent she loves and that they have just become
grandparents. In this fashion, the starting point of the
drama, at first glance, seems no different from its outcome: Florent and Esther remain together because

9. Ibid., p. 49.

they are the same kind of person, and their reality,
through an intricate process of acts and lies, appears
to resume as it was before. Each incident, however, is
subject to double interpretation, for nothing that
took place was necessarily spontaneous, and it is
impossible to discern what is the natural and what is
the contrived. Even Esther and Florent's marriage
may very well represent an unconscious striving
toward an esthetically pleasing existence, a striving
that became such a normal way of life that each
person actually forgot he was playing a part in the
drama he would like his life to become. Games in *Les
Monstres* take on the same qualities as the real: by
the end, every phrase and every gesture is both true
and false. The characters attempt to have better control of the situations in which they find themselves
by playing instead of by proceeding directly. As a
structural reflection of a complex universe, action is
mediate rather than immediate. Moreover, by his constant alternation between the theater and the real,
Cocteau suggests that there is little or no difference
between fact and game, that what man assumes to be
sincerity or truth is only one side of a complicated
puzzle. It is unclear where fiction ends and truth—even
within the framework of the action on stage—begins.
When the curtain opens, the audience sees one actress (whoever plays Esther) pretending to be another
actress (the character Esther). Then the actress who
portrays Liane is one more degree removed from the
spectator because she represents not only an actress
but also an actress playing a role. Such ambiguity
continues with each of the principal characters until
any differentiation between the parts they play in

Les Monstres sacrés and the parts they choose for
themselves within the course of the work is obliter-
ated. The question remains whether there is ever an
actor simply playing a part, or whether there is always a second play unfolding within the first.

   Bacchus, like *Les Monstres sacrés,* raises the question
of the distinction between a role and reality. The
peasant Hans, when he was young, had been chased
and tortured by a group of children from the town's
elite families. Deciding that his only protection
against the vulnerability caused by his poverty was to
feign madness, he pretended to lose his reason as a
consequence of the experience, and everyone actually
believed him to be a half-wit. In his village the towns-
people held an annual festival during which they
elected a young man ("Bacchus") ruler with absolute
power for seven days. Since disorder and tragedy had
previously resulted from the celebration, representa-
tives of the church and government decided that
electing Hans would be their wisest course of action,
because they thought they could control him easily.
Ironically, since he has been such a convincing idiot,
he will have the opportunity to avenge himself and
will be able to reassume his identity. In the course of
the play, illusion or games become truth on two
levels. First, throughout his life Hans's disguise had
been so effective that the townspeople had accepted
him for what he pretended to be. Second, although
according to custom an effigy of the Bacchus or
leader is to be set on fire on the last day of the festivities as an indication of an end to license and a return
to order, in this case Hans himself is put to death at
the close of his reign. Therefore, in another game-

reality reversal, Hans, by "playing" Bacchus, transformed the town's yearly fantasy into something
tragically real. In the place of nonmalicious if raucous
escapades, he substituted a deep threat to the very
way of life in the town. Whereas previous rulers
followed a tradition of anarchy as it were, he made
the anarchy genuine, he challenged the political heritage of the community. Since he overstepped the
boundaries of a game, since he made it real or serious,
he had to face the consequences not of a prank but of
a crime. For a time at least, his roles gave him power,
they triumphed over the reality of those who saw him
as what he pretended to be. A constant alternation
and transposition of facts with make-believe, a perpetual shifting in definitions of truth underscore the
unstable, illusory, fragmented nature of what, in our
simplistic way, we usually call the "real."

In *L'Aigle à deux têtes*, a young widowed queen
strives to create a tragedy in which she can be the
outstanding figure. Taking advantage of the tenth
anniversary of her husband's death, she prepares a
dinner for him. As if destined, a young anarchist
trying to kill her flees into her room in order to avoid
the police. That he looks exactly like the dead king
and has been wounded in the same place is a final
impetus to her plans. As Cocteau explained at the
time he wrote the play, he was fascinated by royalty
who found reality insufficient and who wanted to
change their lives into works of art:

*Il y a très longtemps que je pense à mettre en scène
l'atmosphère de ces familles royales où la folie de
l'art qu'elles n'arrivent pas à mettre en oeuvre les*

*pousse soit à proteger des artistes, soit, faute de
mieux, à faire de leurs vies des drames lyriques.*[10]

One of the essential problems of the play, then, is the
extent to which the queen actually forms her own
life, to what degree her creations affect the givens of
her existence, for at every turn forces apparently prevail over her and direct the course of events in spite
of her:

*'Elle ne pouvait meme pas compter sur le hasard, car
il ya des vies sans hasard.' C'est le style de ma reine.
Elle rêve d'un destin qui lui vienne de l'extérieur,
mais elle décide, elle dirige, elle se mêle de son sort. Il
est probable qu'elle dérange les lignes de sa main
gauche avec la manie de tout décider qu'elle porte
dans sa main droite. Le problème est de savoir si
c'est là son destin ou si elle s'en invente un autre.
C'est la grande énigme. Celle du libre arbitre que les
souverains confondent avec le 'bon plaisir.'*[11]

Freud's ideas became influential in France during
the early years of the century, and since Cocteau was
in contact (albeit sometimes hostile contact) with the
surrealists, it is not surprising that the realms of
dreams and the subconscious should emerge in his
theater as one of the levels coexistent with the everyday. Like the surrealists, he would argue that dreams
capture a different but equally valid component of
the real: they extend consciousness, reflect what it
alone cannot grasp, hence open previously inaccessible realms of knowledge. In conventional speech
"dream" connotes the opposite of reliability—dreams

10. Quoted in
Jean-Pierre Vivet,
"Une reine et un
anarchiste sont
les héros de
*L'Aigle à deux
têtes* de Jean
Cocteau," *Com-
bat,* September
12, 1946.
11. Cocteau, "Ma
Pièce *L'Aigle à
deux têtes* est un
drame du destin,"
Figaro, April 2,
1946.

12. Cocteau,
Théâtre I, p.
276.

somehow do not have the credibility of waking
experiences. During the third act of *La Machine
infernale*, however, Jocasta does not want to sleep
because she is afraid of what she might say while she
is not alert. Isolated in their private nightmares,
Oedipus and Jocasta relive the parts of their lives that
they dare not tell each other. Oedipus is faced with
Anubis, who mocks him; he mutters the Sphinx's
counting and shouts his own fear before the monster.
Jocasta shrinks from "cette pâte immonde,"[12] the
memory of the child she thinks she has had put to
death. Therefore, reality in its most complete form
becomes clear only with the added dimension provided
by dreams: Oedipus is a coward and his mother is
tortured by guilt for a crime that was never committed. Paradoxically, consciousness suppresses truth,
and the subconscious at times allows it to come to
light. In an ironic twist, when one character observes
the dream of the other, because he himself is conscious, he cannot grasp the implications of what he
sees: his consciousness excludes him from breaking a
code decipherable only by the subconscious, because
the latter accurately reflects states of being that can
manifest themselves consciously only as intuitions or
vague, undefined fears.

While dreams in *Les Chevaliers de la Table Ronde*
do not primarily underscore the role of the subconscious, they nevertheless make evident a juxtaposition
of layers of reality which usually remain invisible. In
the second act of the play, for example, Lancelot and
Ségramor, his son, have been sent to Merlin the Socer-
er's *chateau noir*. When the two knights arrive, they
are exhausted from lack of sleep and pass constantly

from a state of consciousness to one of dreams. Their
alternation between one and the other slowly reveals
to them that the criteria for determining truth are not
always the same; in Lancelot's words: "Je pense qu'il
devient difficile, ici, de savoir ce qui est de la réalité
ou du rêve."[13] In one instance, not aware that Lancelot is asleep, Ségramor tells him that his (Ségramor's)
falcon was killed when he first entered the castle.
When Lancelot awakens, he turns to his son, by this
time asleep, and relates the dream he just had: he
saw the little falcon being suffocated by a white
gloved hand. In his dream, then, he learned the truth
not apparent to Ségramor, who was awake at the time
of the incident. Then, waiting for the boy to wake
up, he wanders to a chess table readied for a game
and moves one of the pieces. Another piece moves by
itself, and the knight decides to play with his invisible
opponent, who becomes angry because he is losing
badly and sweeps the pieces from the board. When
Ségramor awakens, he tells his father he dreamed
about him: he saw him playing chess with a handsome
young knight who became enraged at losing and
threw the pieces from the table. Moreover, the young
man was wearing white gloves, the right one of which
was spotted with blood. Ségramor concludes, "Dans
mon rêve, comprenez-vous, je savais, je savais que
c'était le sang de mon pauvre faucon."[14] In his sleep,
the son learned what he and his father could not see
while they were awake: the lord of the castle remains
invisible to ordinary men unless they are asleep. It
is as if the realms—magical and everyday—that operate
in the framework of the play have contact only in
dreams (like the subconscious, they represent

13. Ibid., p. 370.
14. Ibid., p. 370.

15. Mircea
Eliade, *Myth
and Reality*
(New York:
Harper Torch-
books, 1963),
pp. 10 ff.

"another side"), as if the discovery of truth has to be
a process relative to the functioning of each component of the system rather than to the whole.

Just as dreams and waking do not have the same
value in every field of reference, the measurement
of time varies according to the perceiver. No absolute
can explain its passage. In *Orphée*, for example, since
death is a kingdom different from life, if an act is
measured by earth standards, it occupies an hour in
hell but a minute on earth, although it is psychologi-
cally the same in each realm. Therefore, to accomplish
her ritual before Orpheus returns, Death must change
her *vitesse*, she must accommodate herself to man's
time by adjusting what she calls her wavelengths.
The most concrete representations of the relativity of
time are the two scenes which take place on earth
while Orphée is in the underworld. Cocteau repeats a
very short sequence between Heurtebise and a mail-
man. To the reader or spectator these scenes are short,
but while they are taking place, the poet has had the
opportunity to go all the way to Hell, find Eurydice,
and return—because time is not reckoned for him as it
is for the dead: he can move at his own rate and
accomplish in a second what they require an hour to
do.

The action of *Renaud et Armide*, as is fitting for a
magic tale, unfolds in a magic garden. According to
Mircea Eliade, the value of time is a factor that differ-
entiates the sacred from the profane, the extraordinary
from the common.[15] Before man's fall into history,
he was immortal; time for him did not exist. Such is
the condition of Armide, who lives in a paradisaical
garden where nothing changes and it is always sum-

mer. Renaud, however, lives in historical time; he
is mortal; he will grow old and die. Therefore, when
the enchantress gives her ring to the king, she is sur-
rendering a part of her nature in order to be like him,
to exist in his world. The difference between the
times in which each of them moves is one of the factors that makes their union impossible. Because
Renaud conceives Armide as eternally young, he
thinks he can return to France, see his wife, and
attend to affairs in his country; he does not realize
that the fairy princess has become like him in respect
to the effects of duration, that she has lost her quality
of endless youth. It is by juxtaposing time and timelessness that Cocteau presents a state which surpasses
man and can never be part of his experience even if it
is part of his mythic heritage.

In *Les Chevaliers* he opposes time and timelessness
in order to contrast a world governed by enchantment
and one based on human "order." While Arthur's
country is under Merlin's spell, the seasons do not
change, there is no difference between night and day:
there is only a feeble light which does not vary. Time
has stopped; existence is as if suspended outside its
passage. After Arthur exiled the sorcerer, however,
Brittany returned to an alternation between light and
darkness, and the land began to flower. Thus life
falls into its usual patterns, subject to time's course
and rhythm. From *Renaud et Armide* and *Les Chevaliers de la Table Ronde* it is evident that for Cocteau
timelessness signifies a state of magic and of grace
where man is not subject to the laws or constraints of
every day; to employ Eliade's terms, it implies a state
outside of history and therefore outside of the mundane.

The word "time" implies to Cocteau not only duration but also a pace or *vitesse* proper to a situation.
Even when *Les Mariés de la Tour Eiffel*, for example,
is read rather than acted, it is clear that he has juxtaposed such *vitesses* as that of the pompous general
and of farce itself, which proceeds with flippant
rapidity. The general's funeral takes place no more
slowly than does the child's outburst. Each incident,
then, has the same value; even death does not stand
out as a solemn affair. In addition, the scenes with
the "son" illustrate Cocteau's belief that such categories as past, present, and future have no meaning.
Just newlyweds, the bride and groom become parents;
without transition the child grows up and wants to
live his life. The action is viewed from such a dis-
tant perspective that chronology has no meaning.

Magic or the supernatural, the subconscious, games,
and different sorts of time illustrate some of the
many hidden—yet juxtaposed—facets that come together to form a reality that is highly problematic for
the observer. For Cocteau the whole of the real (which
resembles a series of semi-autonomous worlds whose
systems of meaning must be translated from one to
the other if anything is to be understood) results not
from an immutable, pre-defined substratum of being
(although this does indeed exist) but, rather, from the
meshing of this substratum with the perceptual framework of each individual consciousness. For this reason,
the major unstated premises which underlie his work
appear to be that the ambiguity of signs (language,
objects) denotes the fragility (perhaps even the non-
existence) of essence in a traditional, metaphysical
sense; that the role of *l'invisible* is paramount insofar

as the nature of reality is concerned; that conventional logic has no validity; and that all communica-
tions depends on manipulation and, consequently,
knowledge is mediated.

Word games of all types lie at the base of Cocteau's
written work. Like the child's toy that yields different images depending upon the position of the light,
the sense of his sentences shifts according to the context and the listener. Puns and ambiguous sounds gen-
erate much of his poetry, and he seems to delight in
whatever is equivocal. Statements such as one of the
epigraphs to *La Machine infernale* ("Les dieux exist-
ent: C'est le diable")[16] or his affirmation in the preface to the *Mariés de la Tour Eiffel* that "le chef élec-
tricien, avec ses réflexions, m'a souvent éclairé la
piéce"[17] characterize his literary productions as a whole:
words themselves are "double," androgynous, trans-
sexual; they have the same structure as reality itself.

In Cocteau's earlier pieces, plays on word meanings
frequently determine the development of the work:
in addition to reflecting an existential stance, linguistic
ambiguity functions as a structural device. In *Les
Mariés*, for example, the battle scene between the boy
and his parents depends on the word *balles*, since the
word (meaning both "balls" and "bullets") evokes
children as well as battles. Later in the play, although
the funeral oration for the General seems properly
respectful in form and tone, the content lies in direct
contrast with sentiments usually expressed at such an
occasion. For example, while praising the old man's
courage, his eulogizer states, "vous ne vous êtes
jamais rendu, même à l'évidence."[18]

Orphée in some ways resembles *Les Mariés* insofar

16. Cocteau, *La Machine infernale* (Paris: Larousse, n.d.), p. 25.
17. Cocteau, *Théâtre I*, p. 15.
18. Ibid., p. 20.

19. Ibid., p. 150.
20. Ibid., p. 129.
21. Ibid., p. 130.

as language is concerned, because the hopping from one level of a word to another provides a comic, light-hearted effect. After Orpheus and his wife returned from the underworld, for example, Eurydice admiringly explained to Heurtebise—who had in fact told the poet the secret of reaching Hell—that her husband had had the ingenious idea of putting on Death's gloves in order to penetrate the mirror. Seemingly making a joke, Heurtebise replied, "C'est ce qu'on appelle, si je ne me trompe, se donner des gants,"[19] which literally means to take the gloves and figuratively to attribute to oneself the success of an affair, something Orpheus has of course done without his wife's knowing it.

On a deeper level, however, the very substance of *Orphée* depends on the nature of language, since much of the play centers around the phrase "Madame Eurydice reviendra des enfers." To Eurydice, the sentence makes no sense. Orpheus, however, preferring to ignore "meaning" because the statement comes from his horse—that is, the unknown—delights in its mystery:

Orphee. *Il s'agit bien de sens. Colle ton oreille contre cette phrase. Ecoute le mystère. 'Eurydice reviendra' serait quelconque—mais Madame Eurydice! Madame Eurydice reviendra—ce reviendra! ce futur! et la chute: des enfers.*[20]

To him, it is "un poème, un poème de rêve, une fleur du fond de la mort."[21] He does not judge it as he would ordinary language, because he feels it is not part of the world he knows. Ironically, although he

ponders it almost continually, he does not grasp its
prophetic cast even when he is about to seek his wife
in hell. Its significance becomes clear only after the
fact: " 'Madame Eurydice reviendra des enfers.'
Et nous qui refusions un sens à cette phrase."[22]
On the other hand, the Bacchantes read not the
words of the phrase but the first letter of each word;
therefore, they interpret it as an insult to the contest
judges. Prediction, insult, nonsense: none of this preexists as an essence of the sentence, as a meaning. No
value preexists, since it appears that in Cocteau's
world signs by themselves are neutral. To have significance, a word must have a context, and a context is
unstable, since it depends on time and space as well as
on the nature of the perceiver.

Word games might be dismissed as mere frivolity on
Cocteau's part were they not symptomatic of a basic
structure repeated in various forms. Objects, for
instance, have exactly the same elusiveness as words.
A glove in *Orphée* is an article of clothing for mortals
but a key to another world for those who have the
privilege of passing from realm to realm. Depending
on one's point of view, a mirror can be simply a mirror, a passageway to the kingdom of the dead, or a
symbol of descent into the self. While it remains on
her finger, Armide's ring protects her. At one point
in time, in one context, the brooch and scarf in *La
Machine infernale* seem merely bothersome. While
Jocasta remarks that her scarf is always strangling her
and that one day it will kill her, while she describes
her brooch as something that "crève l'oeil à tout le
monde,"[23] the dualism of words intertwines with that
of objects. The Queen thinks she is using language

22. Ibid., p. 149.
23. Ibid., p. 226.

24. Ibid., p. 151.
25. Ibid., p. 157.

figuratively, whereas what she says is literally true: in the gods' system, her jewelry plays the role of an instrument of destruction.

Such ambiguity persists even at the level of the play itself as a system of signs. In *Orphée*, for example, the word "lune" recurs frequently in one scene. Since Eurydice before her marriage had belonged to the Bacchantes, a group of moon-worshipers, and since the Bacchantes had supposedly tricked Orpheus with the horse in order to destroy him, it is not surprising that the poet should take the word out of context and interpret it as a provocation each time Eurydice uses it. When she insists that she has changed a great deal because of her experience in the underworld, she says that she will from now on be "une épouse de lune de miel."[24] Her husband makes her promise never to utter the word again, but while he is complaining about the inconvenience of not being allowed to look at her, she exclaims, "Que veux-tu mon pauvre chéri, tu es toujours dans la lune . . ."[25] Obviously, these stock phrases exacerbate Orphée's impatience, since they appear to indicate that the Bacchantes still control Eurydice without her being fully aware of it. Evidently, then, the word is "double." In addition, however, the French word "lune" in slang means "fesses"—that is, "buttocks." In the context of a largely homosexual audience, at one level the play can become a kind of private experience during which some groups understand allusions of which others are unaware: from a certain point of view, misogyny becomes the center of the work (women destroy the creator Orpheus, women attempt to destroy the artist's inspiration), and the jokes are

fully understood only by a limited number of spectators. Subject matter aside, the same thing is true in
Les Chevaliers when Ginifer assumes Guenièvre's
form and begins to lisp as he makes erotically admiring
remarks about Galaad. Throughout the work, Ginifer's
relationship with Arthur appears at least latently
homosexual, and some of the scenes closely resemble
sketches like "Je l'ai perdue." Analagously, the slick
dialogue and "mod" techniques of *La Machine infernale* constitute the entirety of the play for some
viewers. The "bedroom scene" in the third act can remain simply a bedroom scene, and the play's humor
depends as much on the audience who sees it (because Cocteau predicated his work on a group who
know both *Oedipus Rex* and the upper-middle class/
aristocratic Parisian circles) as it does on anything in
the text itself. *Les Monstres sacrés* can be interpreted
on a purely Boulevard level. The networks of signs
composing these plays take on different values
according to who deciphers the code.

In Cocteau's world, it appears, the sign is a crossroads; hence, it is always double. The same object or
word can exist at the same time in any of the infinite
layers that comprise our reality: the subconscious,
death, or what we call everyday existence. However,
in each layer the sign may have a different value, and
it is not by knowing what something means now that
one can know what it meant a century ago; likewise,
simply understanding the function of a knife or a
glove in the course of one's daily life does not imply
understanding its function in a dream or in another
society. Most of the time, unfortunately, because we
do not realize that other standards for judgments

exist, the greater part of reality remains invisible to
us. Like the surrealists, Cocteau attributed some of
this blindness to our being culture-bound. As children
we perceived in a nondistorted, natural way because
we had not been programmed by society, but as we
grew up, we gradually learned to arrange data only in
the forms provided by language, class, and nationality.
In his theoretical as well as fictional writings, Cocteau
frequently argued that one can see only what he has
been taught to see. In *Orphée* Death moves about on
earth disguised as an elegant woman, for if she looked
as everyone expected her to look—if she manifested
herself as a culturally accepted image of Death—people
would recognize her and hinder her work. Inversely,
when the Sphinx in *La Machine infernale* asked
Anubis why the god of the dead has assumed the
shape that credulous human beings think he has,
Anubis replied that the god would remain invisible
unless he appeared to men as they imagined him.
Only "simple"—that is, childlike—people who have
not shut out the complexity of existence in order to
adopt the truth dictated by society have access to
the domain of the supernatural or of dreams. Only
they can understand that games and fact do not
essentially differ. On another level, Armide's remaining a fairy kept her invisible—even when she
attempted to appear—because the signs that evoked
"woman" in her magic realm were incomprehensible
to Renaud. A central problem represented in Cocteau's production, therefore, is the epistemological
one of dealing with the invisible, for often the universe appears to be nothing but an elaborate camou-
flage system. For this reason almost every work takes

the form of an initiation rite during which the chara-
ters suffer until they learn—too late, for the most
part—how to decipher codes.

The traditional occidental tool for problem-solving
is syllogistic logic, which implies a belief in what
Hume called causal connections. The basic assumption underlying confidence in syllogistic reasoning is
that the terms of the premises are related, and, consequently, valid conclusions can be drawn from them.
When, however, as in Cocteau's world, the meaning
of signs depends completely on context, and when
context (being often invisible) cannot be determined,
the acceptance of any kind of necessary relationship
between two propositions becomes untenable. As an
attack against the simplistic, pretentious bases on
which most human beings organize their lives—especially the premise that everything can be known and
therefore controlled—Cocteau presented commonplace situations arranged associationally rather than
causally. Although there is no evidence that he had
ever read Hume's works, he apparently would have
accepted the British philosopher's argument that
man's experience rather than some immutable prop-
erty in matter itself leads him to arrange a series of
events always in the same fashion.

The characters in *Le Boeuf sur le toit*, for example,
have their source in the image a Frenchman might
have of an American speakeasy during Prohibition:

*Entrent tour à tour: la dame décolletée, en robe
rouge, très maniérée, très commune. La dame rousse,
aux cheveux de papier, jolie, d'allure masculine, un
peu voûtée, les mains dans les poches. Le monsieur*

26. Cocteau,
Théâtre II,
p. 598.

*en habit de moleskine, qui regarde son bracelet-
montre et ne quitte plus son tabouret de bar
jusqu'à sa sortie. Un bookmaker écarlate, aux dents
d'or, qui porte un melon gris et une cravate de
chasse maintenue par une perle de la taille d'une
boule de jardin.*[26]

Moreover, all the violence associated with the era
sets the work in motion: *La Dame rousse* seduces the
boxer whom the bookmaker knocks unconscious because they are both interested in the same woman.
With the arrival of the policeman, the bar sells milk
instead of drinks and the barman kills the officer by
lowering a fan which decapitates him. Seen from afar,
in a perspective where violence is unimportant because it takes place in a dream world, the action
becomes increasingly farcical and proceeds by associations that are comprehensible only within the context of the plot, since nothing follows necessarily
from anything preceding it. Since the policeman was
decapitated, for example, *La Dame rousse* dances
with his head as if she were Salome, and since she is
in a bar, she shakes the head as if it were a cocktail
shaker. Because the action is farcical and can't have
an unhappy ending, the barman resuscitates the
officer after the others have left and presents him
with a bill ten feet long. The general activity of a
speakeasy, then, is not a closed unit: using exactly
the same elements—barman, bookmaker, speakeasy,
red headed woman—Cocteau could have related them
in an infinite number of ways. He could have chosen
a serious rather than a comic tone. While the associational links he made are comprehensible, they are not

predictable; they are not necessary or causal on any
other than a personal level: nothing inherent in the
acts of decapitiation and dancing forces someone un-
familiar with the Bible and opera to think of Salome.

Like *Le Boeuf sur le toit, Les Mariés de la Tour
Eiffel* develops through a series of associations
growing out of a familiar situation. In addition, it
presents a much less subtle destruction of traditional
reasoning, since the play's construction, as we explained earlier, is bipartite. While one proposition of
the syllogism lies in the world of every day, the other
belongs to a magical realm. The camera's malfunc-
tioning transforms the inevitable picture-taking at a
bourgeois wedding into a fantastic event: it is as if the
"birdie's" disappearance were a signal that more than
one sign system had entered into play. Because the
bird flew away, something else must emerge whenever
the photographer says, "Un oiseau va sortir": hence,
the bathing beauty, child, and lion. The child is
"naturally" associated with the newlyweds and becomes their future offspring. Because one prediction
about him is that he will be "un beau petit mort
pour la prochaine guerre,"[27] he looks in his basket for
balles, the balls/bullets which massacre his family.
Likewise, the lion is associated with the general because the latter had earlier told stories about Africa,
where he saw tigers that looked like wasps because of
a mirage. He, of course, "logically" comes to the conclusion that the lion he sees must be a mirage because
it is on the Eiffel Tower. In this manner the inapplica-
bility of traditional logic becomes apparent: the
general has reasoned with a tool which has nothing
in common with the magic that is his sphere of reality,

27. Cocteau,
Théâtre I, p. 17.

and therefore he cannot deduce correctly. By definition, a syllogism cannot function with unrelated terms. The old man's blindness (similar to Orpheus' or Arthur's or Oedipus') reflects mankind's general inability to deal with anything outside his expectations or his mental sets. Oblivious to the invisible, he persists in treating everything around him as if it were homogeneous.

Insofar as creative process was concerned—and this no doubt helps explain the structures in his work— Cocteau apparently proceeded associationally. When questioned in an interview as to the source of some of his characters, like Anubis in *La Machine*, he replied that much of what he had done was based on images from his childhood, from things that impressed him and were dear to him. In such a highly personal artistic universe, it is not surprising that communication should be effected evocatively through verbal and graphic images rather than through a more scientific type of discourse. Judging from Cocteau's work as a whole, one must deduce that communication results only from skillful manipulation and that, by extension, the acquisition of knowledge is of necessity mediated.

As we have shown, the Coctelian universe is composed by overlapping spheres, and each one appears to have its own language or system of signs. Passing from one level to the other depends on a series of calculations similar to translation. When Death and her companions come for Eurydice, they use complicated steps and tools to transfer the young woman from one state to another: they adjust wave lengths as they draw Eurydice's soul toward them on a kind

of metaphoric "thread of life." Moreover, to be able
to move about accurately among the living, Death has
to have machinery which compensates for the fact
that she does not perceive as mortals do, she does not
see things exactly where they see them. Orphée's
entering the kingdom of the Dead would be impossible without the mirror and the glove: one must
possess a key in order to understand.

Since art and acting for Cocteau participated in an
order of reality different from that of everyday,
communication from stage to audience depended on
calculated evocation rather than on direct statement.
In *Orphée*, for example, Death is represented by a
group of signs rendered meaningful by certain cultural
associations an audience might make. For French
spectators the conception of Death as a woman could
be explicable merely by the word "la mort." Other
details appear to have had their origins in Cocteau's
personal impressions, and the transition from a
private to a public language could be made only
through the use of connotation. Death's elegant
dress, her equipment and machinery, her aides, their
ritualistic steps—all suggest a view that integrates the
new with the traditional: while the mystery of Death
remains, the gadgetry and scientific paraphernalia of
the twentieth century also have their place, since
they in fact represent a different kind of mystery or
command another sort of awe. Whatever the case, Cocteau's synthesizing of diverse elements (such as the
complex series of associations he had with death)
required a vehicle or a mediating device—usually in
the form of either a verbal or a visual image—in order
to be expressed.

The view of the world that one can deduce from these characteristics of Cocteau's work and the impression that emerges from his techniques are essentially ones of fragmentation. On every level—personal, social, cosmic—existence appears to be split, since all "truth" depends on time and perspective. Therefore, the doubles or masks that form the core of Cocteau's work summarize his basic existential stance. When he states, for example, that he is a lie that always tells the truth (a statement that has provoked endless criticism on the ground of its frivolity), and when he explains that by "lie" he means the social self or the persona behind which one hides, he is not, it seems, merely being clever. He follows, rather, as a descendant of Rimbaud's discovery that "I" is another, that the self is not a coherent, unified whole. Any number of factors might explain Cocteau's acute consciousness of ambiguity: his being homosexual in a society whose typical members condemned such a thing; his frequenting individuals (often aristocratic) who had more money than he and upon whom he became dependent financially; most generally, his existing during a period and in a milieu riddled by the kind of contradictions that produced the Dreyfus affair as well as by the deep social problems responsible for French indecisiveness in the 1930's. It appears that Cocteau was placed in the position of pretending to be what he was not, of hiding what he was, until the very mode of his existence became an unstable series of games and masks, and he himself was never completely and simply one.

In such a universe, subjectivity emerged as the most significant element. In Cocteau's view, all meaning and all value have their source in the perceiving consciousness rather than in the object itself. Moreover, abstractions like justice or unknowable phenomena like death have no existence outside the mind: they are human creations. In a sense the world is nothing but appearance, nothing but systems of signs constructed to elicit responses; and behind these signs, these clusters that we have learned to interpret the way we do because of our culture or our personality, no independent essence exists. Hence all of art (in fact all of life whose form art imitates) can ultimately be comprised only of masks or games—of things contrived to look as they should. In a conversation with Jean-Louis Barrault, Jean-Paul Sartre, and Jean Vilar about the stage, Cocteau once remarked that "pour les pièces modernes, le vrai langage est un faux langage naturel, il doit avoir l'air d'un langage naturel."[28] The key phrase is, of course, *avoir l'air*, since everything in Cocteau's universe must be played out by manipulating signs. Rather than being natural, language—by extension, all modes of communication—has to be arranged in such a fashion that the audience perceives it as natural. The indirectness that characterizes Cocteau's work derives from a never explicitly stated disbelief in a stable core of meaning or of existence. One can never depict directly what does not exist (some sort of essense); one can only draw upon configurations that look "as if." The perpetual use of images, puns, games, and mirrors in his work results not from superficial attempts at virtuosity but from a deep intuition (comic as well as tragic) of a contingent reality in flux.

Two of the key words that can be used to describe

28. Jean-Paul Sartre, *Un Théâtre de situations* (Paris: Gallimard Collections, Idées), 1973, p. 45.

Cocteau's universe, therefore, are "deceive" and "deception": at every moment the public finds itself surrounded by a web of game and untruth. A large proportion of "the invisible" in Cocteau's work remains hidden because of deception in the form of masks, disguises or other doubles. In *Orphée* the angel Heurtebise pretends to be a glazier, and Death dresses as an elegant woman. In *Les Chevaliers* Merlin tries to pass for an honorable *aumônier*, and Ginifer plays at imitating whomever the occasion calls for. Examining farther, however, one realizes that none of this can be interpreted merely as occasional deception. Instead, the nature and structure of the universe revolve inescapably around trickery (after all, we are deceived into believing in essence and meaning)—hence the importance of the word "machine," which for Cocteau implies a sort of calculated, inalterable functioning.

From Death's mechanized ritual in *Orphée* to the telephone in *La Voix humaine* and Oedipus' intricate destruction in *La Machine infernale*, machines and mechanical devices form one of the constants in Cocteau's art. Like his virtuosity, his use of machinery is far from gratuitous and has ramifications greatly surpassing a literal presence on the stage. The processes as well as the structure of his universe operate mechanistically: there is no chance, no accident. At the same time, interestingly enough, there is no teleology: the course of events does not tend ultimately toward anything specific. While Cocteau evidently played upon the archetype of the persecuted poet or of the damned superior human being—society's scapegoat—he nevertheless did not depict this phe-

nomenon as personalized and angry; rather, the way
of the world, almost completely detached from any
human control, is such that what Cocteau called "the
great disorders" (which manifest themselves in outstanding human beings) are necessarily suppressed
when they appear in history. To use an image that
occurs frequently in Cocteau's writings, having somehow been "written" in the first three dimensions,
whatever "happens" simply unfolds in the fourth dimension, time.

In addition to functioning like a machine, the
universe is constructed like one: each component
moves only at the appropriate moment, and the
placing of elements is tightly controlled. The analogy
Cocteau frequently draws upon to evoke the world's
structure is the kaleidoscope:

*Il est possible qu'en inventant le kaléidoscope on ait
mis le doigt sur un grand secret. Car ses combinaisons
infinies proviennent de trois éléments en apparence
étrangers les uns aux autres. Une rotation. Des bouts
de verre. Un miroir.*[29]

The reality that provided the fabric of his work
clearly resembles this kaleidoscope metaphor and, by
extension, astronomy models, since elements can
appear, it seems, only at certain times and become
visible only in certain circumstances. Moreover, they
are refracted and interpreted (rather than simply reflected or absorbed) by consciousness. Such concepts
help explain much of the problem of invisibility.
Oedipus, for example, remains blind to all the signs
around him (signs evident to the spectators, since

29. Cocteau, *Jour-
nal d'un inconnu*
(Paris: Grasset,
1953), p. 25.

they perceive at a different chronological point from
the king) because it is not yet time that he see: the
components he needs in order to understand his
dilemma do not shift into a configuration he is able
to decipher until he has already committed his crimes.
In essence, Oedipus' curse does not depend on the
fact that he is denied knowledge or that he is not permitted to understand: rather, it is written that he
should learn to read too late. In addition to the inherent ambiguity and flux of all things (consequently
of all signs), which prevent human beings from de-
coding their environments, the processes of life deceive them in the very course of things. One has to
contend not only with an elusive reality but also with
a relentless machine: there is no god of mercy to
whom one can appeal; there is no hope to change
events. Throughout Cocteau's theater, the image of
the machine dominates in many forms. His literal
representation of machines, his use of language and of
dramatic irony, and the structure of his plays all
underscore the presence of controlling forces and
create works of art that are themselves machines.

In some plays Cocteau makes the presence of controlling forces outside the characters explicit by using
a literal machine such as the typewriter in *La Machine
à écrire* and the telephone in *La Voix humaine*. The
woman in *La Voix humaine*, for example, is totally
dependent upon the functioning of the instrument:
every time the connection breaks or the noise becomes
unbearable, she is in danger of not being able to communicate with her lover in their final conversation.
Since the wires are the only link between the two
people, they ultimately have control over them. In

Orphée the horse is in fact a *machine à poésie* which leads to Orpheus' dismemberment. The machinery of *Les Mariés de la Tour Eiffel* operates on two levels. On the first, the *appareil détraqué* obviously has power over the wedding party. On the second, phonographs that narrate the action are even more important. Since the voices are supposedly on records, they themselves have no liberty; they must say what has been recorded. This implies that the characters act out something that has already been determined, that the whole incident is planned rather than spontaneous. Even the camera is not really out of order, it is only following the role dictated to it. Therefore, at the end of the sketch, the phonographs give cues for the actor's exit and signal the closing of the Tower.

In many plays and in almost all of Cocteau's poetry, the spoken word assumes power and resembles a cog or functioning unit in a mechanical device. Like a *déclic* or a starting mechanism, particular sounds can cause events to take place. For example, simply the word *balles* in *Les Mariés de la Tour Eiffel* provoked the massacre scene with the little boy. Without their knowing it, the characters' references to violence made violence inevitable. One might say they stumbled upon a secret expression or password. A similar phenomenon occurs toward the end of the play when the family has posed for its wedding picture. The phonographs describe their pose in terms of a painting:

Phono Deux. *Regardez. La noce et le photographe se figent. La noce est immobile. Ne la trouvez-vous pas un peu . . .*

30. Cocteau,
Théâtre I, p. 22.
31. Ibid., p. 250.

Phono Un. *Un peu gateux.*
Phono Deux. *Un peu bouquet.*
Phono Un. *Un peu Joconde.*
Phono Deux. *Un peu chef-d'oeuvre.*[30]

The art dealer and collector who enter actually take
the group for a painting and discuss it as if it were a
work of art: the phonographs' description has made
it one.

   In *La Machine infernale, Renaud et Armide,* and
Les Chevaliers de la Table Ronde, language assumes
the power of incantation. It seems as if certain combinations or rhythms of words are magic, as if they
can control by their charms. Through them an unknown force acquires mastery over human beings. In
La Machine infernale the Sphinx paralyzes Oedipus
with her speech:

Le Sphinx. *Et je parle, je travaille, je dévide, je
    déroule, je calcule, je médite, je tresse, je vanne,
    je tricote, je natte, je croise, je passe, je repasse,
    je noue et dénoue et renoue, retenant les moin-
    dres noeuds qu'il me faudra te dénouer ensuite
    sous peine de mort . . .*[31]

The repetition and intonations act as a hypnotizing
agent, quelling the victim's resistance. Armide's magic
formulae are chanted in a ritualistic manner. As she
traps Renaud in an imaginary web, her voice becomes
a literal thread winding closer and closer about him,
until it imprisons him:

Fil, fil, fil, sur mon coeur enroule ta pelote. Sors de

moi, fil, fil, fil. Fil qui cours, fil qui flottes, De cet homme orgueilleux regarde le profil. Tisse autour de Renaud ta toile, fil, fil, fil.[32]

32. Cocteau,
Théâtre II, p. 213.
33. Cocteau,
Théâtre I, p. 391.

Likewise, Merlin the Sorcerer in *Les Chevaliers* draws a great portion of his power from his knowledge of magic chants which can transfer him anywhere and change the appearance of those around him:

Cinq et cinq ne font plus dix
Au nom du singe et du fils
Au nom de la salamandre
Par la flamme et par la cendre
En amont et en aval.
Que la reine soit cheval.[33]

A special case of his use of language, dramatic irony was one of the most effective techniques by which Cocteau presented different perspectives of the same situation while he revealed that his characters were ignorant of factors directing their lives. They use expressions or state opinions whose significance they grasp only partially: they accept the figurative meaning of a phrase, for example, when its literal meaning is the correct description of their predicment. Only at the end of the play do they realize the limits of their experience and of their understanding. Thus, the multiple connotations of a word not only reflect the numerous levels of the real but in addition underscore the elements of the whole that have not yet entered the characters' line of vision. A comic instance of dramatic irony occurs, of course, in *Orphée* when the poet returns from hell with Eurydice and

34. Ibid., p. 149.

says to Heurtebise:

Orphee. *Mon cher, vous êtes un ange.*
Heurtebise. *Pas du tout.*
Orphee. *Si, si, un ange, un vrai ange. Vous m'avez sauvé.*[34]

Obviously, the play that depends to the greatest extent upon dramatic irony as a reflection of a mechanistic universe is *La Machine infernale*. The ambiguous language (sliding from the literal to the figurative with equal validity on both levels) highlights the crucial position of time, since the spectator has access to Oedipus' perspective in addition to his own: the two horizons of knowledge are juxtaposed before him. No matter what the king and Jocasta did, they could not see: the dualistic allusions to the brooch and scarf, Jocasta's flirting with young soldiers and her extolling the ideal state of the mother-son relationship, Oedipus' feeling of having "returned home," the exclamations of "she's old enough to be his mother," remain uncomprehended until all the components, all the cogs finally move into the suitable position. The precautions and reasonings of the two major characters yield nothing, then, because the forces of the universe make it impossible for them to comprehend.

Judging from Cocteau's work, we must conclude that the most accurate summary of his world-view appears to be Anubis' description in *La Machine infernale*: an infinite series of overlapping spheres which control those within them. Such a comparison accounts for the elusiveness of reality (since the per-

ceiver often doesn't know that he must translate signs
from one realm to another and since translation itself
may at times be impossible) as well as for its predetermined, mechanistic nature. In his plays this basic
framework manifests itself structurally on two levels.
First, the architecture of each work depends on a
utilization of well-known motifs whose functioning
resembles the kaleidoscope-like elements that form
the base of the real. Second, each play has the form
of a play-within-a-play and hence reflects the dualism
inherent in existence. Likewise, novels such as *Les
Enfants terribles* or *Thomas l'Imposteur* develop as
games-within-games.

Cocteau's detractors have often remarked that he
did not invent a single one of his plays, and it can
hardly be denied that he drew heavily on—and in fact
often literally transposed—Greek tragedy for his own
purposes. The Greeks were not his only source of
established motifs, however. He borrowed other
patterns which were just as familiar to his audience
and just as well defined. In addition to myths such as
those of Antigone, Oedipus, or Orpheus and classical works such as Racine's *Phèdre* or Shakespeare's
Romeo and Juliet, he borrowed from folklore,
legends, and fables: *Le Pauvre matelot, Les Chevaliers
de la Table Ronde, Reanud et Armide,* and *L'Ecole
des veuves* are based on the lore of the Middle Ages,
on fairy tales, and on popular traditions or tales. *Les
Parents terribles* combined boulevard drama with the
Oedipus legend, and *L'Aigle à deux têtes*, with its
foreboding atmosphere, two suicides, and love between a queen and a commoner captured the essence
of Romantic melodrama.

35. Quoted in
Benjamin Cré-
mieux, "Jean
Cocteau et *La
Machine infer-
nale," Je Suis
Partout*, April 28,
1934.

Even in the works that Cocteau adapted almost without alteration, the myths or motifs composing their core became structural blocks in the building of his own universe. He constructed works that were a microcosm of his mental structures. For example, motifs repeated throughout his work mirrored his intuition of a hidden but eternal return of the elements that composed the machine. The characteristic of motifs that appealed to Cocteau—their recurring in many forms while they retained a stable core—reflected his fascination with the kaleidoscope, since in his work a small number of constants appear with endless variations, distortions, and combinations. Haunted by the many faces of reality, he adapted the same configurations in many ways, a technique that highlighted both the illusory nature of truth and its inalterable components. In addition, what gives his creations the quality of "un toboggan emportant d'un trait, dans un glissement impossible à freiner, le public vers le rire ou les larmes,"[35] is the motifs which constitute their base. Through the years, certain patterns have acquired a stability that makes them easily recognized by the public. For example, if the characters in a play consist of an old husband, his young wife, and their young male guest, the result is always catastrophic for the husband, because the two young people fall in love. Since the requirements of genre also determine its path, tone and significance will vary according to whether the work is a comedy or a tragedy but, like a predetermined mechanism that has only to function in the same way it has many times before, it progresses to its inevitable outcome. Thus a motif is itself a machine and at the same time represents a component of the world-machine. The sure development of his plays depended on his having chosen premises which, in the logic of the theater, invariably entailed the same conclusions.

36. Cocteau, *Théâtre I*, p. 204.

Among Cocteau's adaptations of classical subjects, only two—*La Machine infernale* and *Orphée*—were altered significantly from the original. Nevertheless, both unfold syllogistically from the myth that is their prototype. Once the reader or spectator becomes aware of the Christian source of *Orpheus* and of its farcical elements, he can predict exactly what will take place. The phrase *Madame Eurydice reviendra des Enfers* alerts him to Eurydice's death, and the Bacchantes' hatred indicates that the poet will be dismembered. The myth thus has an identity that cannot be altered. In the same manner, after two deaths the presence of a guardian angel foreshadows a resurrection, especially in a farce. Moreover, in Cocteau's opinion, the likelihood of a motif's recurring at any era or in any civilization underscored the durability of legend, just as its predictable unfolding implied a predetermined course.

As the well-known prologue in *La Machine infernale* shows, Cocteau did nothing but step back in time so that he might depict the processes of the gods' order as well as its result:

Regarde, spectateur, remontée à bloc, de telle sorte que le ressort se déroule avec lenteur tout le long d'une vie humaine, une des plus parfaites machines construites par les dieux infernaux pour l'anéantissement mathématique d'un mortel.[36]

37. Ibid., p. 78.

Since the subject of the play is the inescapable accomplishment of what has already been decided, the work essentially presents the steps between what is "given" in a mathematical proof and what these statements imply. When the curtains open, Laius has already been murdered, because his death insures the fulfillment of the remainder of the prophecy.

Although not patterned on a familiar classical drama, the situation of *La Voix humaine* is nonetheless firmly established in a more popular tradition. Cocteau simplified the action as much as possible by eliminating details both of the ending affair and of the impending wedding. Moreover, he emphasized that the mistress is "une victime médiocre,"[37] that she is merely repeating a role that is played every day. Finally, he arranged the scene in such a manner that nothing could prevent its dénouement. The whole of the plot consists of the last telephone conversation between the rejected woman and her lover who has called at her request. It is as if Cocteau chose a point as close as possible to the end of the relationship so that there would be only an infinitesimal step from his premises to his conclusion. Thus when the mistress learns by accident that her lover is not at home, as he declared, but instead at the apartment of his fiancée, the last piece falls into place. Nothing can be reversed, because the cycle has come to its end.

The mechanisms that direct Cocteau's later plays are much more complex than those of his first attempts at dramatic creation. Whereas *La Voix humaine*, for example, unfolded in a strictly linear fashion, *Les Parents terribles, Renaud et Armide,* and *L'Aigle à deux têtes* depend on a conflict of arche-

types and motifs. The logic of *Les Chevaliers de la
Table Ronde* and *Bacchus* derives in part from the
author's personal mythology but belong also to a
larger, more accessible system. In the later plays,
though characters remain mechanical dolls, they are
not homogeneous and they are caught in intricate
situations which force their "givens" toward crisis.
Each work, therefore, groups and contrasts pre-
defined forces that struggle toward resolution.

Les Parents terribles is constructed on three tri-
angular relationships, each of which operates according to well-established theatrical conventions. The
triangle which generates the play itself is that of
Georges, his wife Yvonne, and his former fiancée
Léo, who is also his sister-in-law and who lives with
the couple. Having decided that, since she lives more
abstractly than concretely, she could not give Georges
the deep love he needed, Léo brought him and her
sister together. Although she and Georges have never
had an affair (as they would have done in a Boulevard
play), Léo is still in love with him. Through the years
she has done everything she can to protect him and to
make his life easier. Therefore, even if her affection,
because of her character, can never manifest itself
physically, her emotions are nevertheless alive. Her
only allegiance stronger than the one to Georges is
the one she has for love itself, the idealized love she
and he could never have.

The second triangle is the essentially tragic one
composed of Georges, Yvonne, and their son Michel.
Yvonne has a savage, possessive love for her child that
excludes everyone else. On the other hand, it appears
that Michel has a normal relationship with her. Like

38. Ibid., p. 457.
39. Ibid., p. 486.

many little boys, he once expressed the desire to
marry his mother, but then he naturally passed beyond
this stage and fell in love with someone his own age.
Just as there is no adultery between Léo and Georges,
there is no incest between Michel and Yvonne, but
in both cases strong emotions lie close to the surface.

The third triangle which, because of the other two,
precipitates a crisis in the family is a deflected Oedipal
relationship which, resulting from a *quiproquo*,
takes the form of a vaudeville episode or, in Georges'
words, a "pièce de Labiche."[38] Ignored by his wife,
who is interested only in her child, Georges takes a
mistress, Madeleine, who is much younger than he.
After spending a night away from home, Michel returns to announce that he intends to marry a young
woman who happens to be, unknown to him, his
father's mistress. Coupled with the second triangle,
the third has an ambiguous quality—of an Oedipal
tragedy and of a farce—which Cocteau developed
simultaneously. For example, one confrontation between Georges and Madeleine summarizes the misunderstanding at the base of *Oedipe-Roi*:

Madeleine. *Si tu m'avais dit ton vrai nom . . .*
Georges. *Tu n'en aurais pas moins rencontré Michel.*
Madeleine. *Je l'aurais evité.*[39]

Moreover, Madeleine is three years older than her
fiancée, she is much more mature than he, and she
has a job and the responsibilities of an adult where he
has none, because he is a child. In addition, she is his
father's mistress. Not marrying his mother, Michel has
nevertheless found someone who virtually occupies

her position in his father's life. On the other hand, these circumstances are also in the tradition of Molière's *Ecole des femmes*, in which the older man in love with a younger woman is ridiculed and repulsed. It must be remembered that Cocteau highlighted the vaudeville, boulevard aspects of *La Machine infernale*. As Taladoire has pointed out, Cocteau was able to balance the tragic and vaudeville aspects of *Les Parents terribles* by drawing upon the structural characteristics common to both genres of theater:

40. B. A. Taladoire, "*Les Parents terribles* de Jean Cocteau," *Cahiers du Sud*, January 1939.

le miracle de cette pièce, c'est d'être à la fois et à chacun des moments de l'action, un vaudeville et une tragédie . . . Le vaudeville et la tragédie s'apparentent en effet, étroitement, par une sorte de fatalité dont le double visage, aux yeux des hommes, est la coincidence et l'enchaînement des événments. Le sens de ces coincidences qui échappent à la vie courante, un poète sait le percevoir, quand il l'est, comme Cocteau, au titre d'humoriste et à celui de dramaturge. Ainsi, l'aspect vaudevillesque d'un sujet peut se developper sous les doigts en même temps que son aspect tragique.[40]

However complicated these interlocking series of events may be, they are premises that entail an inevitable conclusion. As we have indicated, Yvonne's attachment to her son is not reciprocated in like manner. He loves her, but not as she loves him; he maintains a close but ordinary mother-child attachment. Similarly, his attraction to Madeleine is "natural," whereas the relation of his father to the girl, like that of Arnolphe and his ward Agnès, is not. It is the

41. Cocteau,
Théâtre I, p.
423.

order of the world, at least on the stage, that sons
leave their mothers to marry and that an older man
loses in love to a younger one. Therefore, Michel and
Madeleine will be united at the end of the play. The
only momentary obstacle is Leonie, who, anxious to
help George, plans a drama to separate them. However, her passion for order, for the ideal of love, is
a priori stronger than her affections for her former
fiancé (or she would have married him herself), and
she corrects her mistake. Consequently, everything
falls into place. Because of her impetuous, emotional
nature, Yvonne commits suicide, although she really
does not want to. She simply reacts without thinking,
as usual, because she understand the inevitability of
what is about to take place—Michel's marriage. Thus
ends the tragic thread of the play.

What Cocteau meant when he said of *Les Parents
terribles* that "les rôles doivent être sacrifiés à la
pièce et la servir au lieu de se servir d'elle,"[41] now
becomes clear. At every stage of the action, at every
decision they make, the characters are in fact reacting to their circumstances instead of creating new
circumstances. They have no power over what is
being accomplished: after the machine is set in
motion, they are only the material it shapes. In turn,
the effect it has on them is determined by what they
are, by the preexistent mechanism of their own personalities. It is the unfolding of the various motifs
which represent the forces at work in the universe
that governs the action.

The story of Renaud and Armide appeared origi-
nally in Tasso's *Gerusalemme Liberata* (1575) and in
the seventeenth century became the subject of a

tragedy by Quinault whose text later formed the
basis of an opera with music by Gluck. Cocteau retained the Italian writer's theme of love and his
atmosphere of enchantment, but omitted his message
of Christian redemption. Described as "un jeu ou de
grands insectes se dévorent et flambent,"[42] *Renaud et
Armide* is a tragic fairy tale in which a magic ring has
decided the heroine's fate long before the start of
the play. In the first act Armide suggests taking off
the ring which makes her invisible so that Renaud
may see her and know her love; but after Oriane, her
suivante, has recited the laws governing all those who
wear it, it becomes evident that the couple's relationship can only be unhappy. Later on, after Renaud
has lost his reason, he appears driven to possess the
ring—that is, to accomplish the one act destined to
destroy the princess. Finally, in his delirium, he sings
the haunting, obsessive, tragic "song" that does not
yet exist, as he says, and that foreshadows an ending
which will follow the action of the play itself:

42. Cocteau/Fraig-
neau, *Entretiens*,
p. 151.
43. Cocteau,
Théâtre II, p. 268.

> *Armide est morte.*
> *Connaissez-vous Renaud que dans la terre on porte?*
> *On couvre Renaud mort avec son écusson.*
> *Connaissez-vous Renaud de la triste chanson?*
> *La chanson de Renaud, le roi qu'on porte en terre.*
> *Elle n'existe pas encore. On doit la taire.*
> *Jusqu'à ce qu'elle existe. On doit la taire. On doit*
> *La taire. La chanson du roi Renaud, du roi*
> *Renaud. Connaissez-vous le roi Renaud, Madame?*
> *Connaissez-vous Armide?*[43]

During the course of the work, then, Cocteau

44. In Pierre-
Aimé Touchard,
"*L'Aigle à deux
têtes.*" *Spectateur,*
February 4, 1947.

deliberately indicates what its outcome will be. It is
as if the great cycle of love, fate, and death are
irrevocably set, as if the two lovers are continuing a
process at work not only in Tasso's episode but also
in *Romeo and Juliette* or *Pelléas et Mélisande.* Even
as the plot unfolds, it seems that the poet is under-
scoring the power of myth.

Although one has the form of a classical tragedy
and the other the style of Romantic melodrama, the
motif and construction of *L'Aigle à deux têtes* and
Renaud et Armide are virtually identical. Describing
L'Aigle to Pierre-Aime Touchard, Cocteau said:

*J'ai voulu écrire une pièce d'un romantisme anti-
romantique et dont le style soit si dur que les acteurs,
s'ils se trompent d'un mot, n'y puissent retrouver
leur équilibre . . .*
    *L'Aigle à deux têtes est rigoureusement construit
comme une fugue. Edwige Feuillère, surprenante de
force et de grace hautaine, en est le premier thème.
Au deuxième acte, c'est le thème de Jean Marais qui
commence. Les thèmes s'épousent, séparés par les
deux charnières des scènes de Jacques Varennes.
Ensuite, les thèmes luttent pour se résoudre dans la
dernière scène ou la double chute des héros figure ce
double accord final.*[44]

Such a statement recalls the structure of *Renaud et
Armide*:

*Si je me suis inspiré de quelque ouvrage, ce serait
plutôt à la musique de théâtre que je serais redev-
able . . . Je parle de la science d'un Gluck et d'un*

Wagner en ce qui concerne l'enchaînement et le développement des thèmes. Orphée, Tristan et Ysolde, *restent les exemples d'un mécanisme ideal de longues et de brèves, de précisions et de cris du coeur.*[45]

45. Cocteau, *Théâtre II*, p. 174.

Cocteau's remarks make quite explicit his conception of the mathematical precision that controls the development of every work.

Only a year after completion of *L'Aigle*, Cocteau adapted *Ruy Blas* for the screen, and it is probable that the Hugo play was in his mind when he composed his own tragedy of love, fate, and death: the impossible union of a commoner and a queen, their ideals of righting a corrupt government, and the inevitable destruction of two superior human beings by the pettiness of others form the axis of its plot. He managed to incorporate within his drama most elements characterizing the Romantic myth of love. For example, at the start of the first act, the Queen reads her destiny in the cards, and by a technique reminiscent of Bizet's *Carmen*, the outcome is immediately made clear. The stormy night, the mysterious appearance of a young anarchist named Azraël (the angel of death) who is the double of the late king, the powerful roles associated with the *monstres sacrés* of Cocteau's childhood memories—each factor recreates not only a world of ill-starred heroes but also the epoch and style of a Bernhardt or of a Mounet-Sully.

Although the denouement of *Bacchus* depends in part on Cocteau's idealization of the Poet, the play nevertheless unfolds in the pattern of an easily recognized motif. Cocteau often stated that Antigone

46. Cocteau/Frai-
gneau, *Entretiens*,
p. 63.

was his saint.[46] To him she represented the artist,
because she rebelled against society's authority in
order to defend what she believed; in his terms, she
remained faithful to herself without regard to social
demands. Like her, Hans in *Bacchus* is an anarchist-
poet. The Cardinal, who resembles Creon, represents
the status quo or the order of the world, whereas
Hans refuses to compromise what he is. He chooses
to remain pure and is murdered at the end of the
play. The guiding motif is the same as in *Antigone*—
the destruction of one who goes against the rules of
his civilization, who breaks its taboos. It repeats the
cycle of the martyr or the saint. Even without
knowing the significance of this myth in Cocteau's
thought, the spectator can probably recognize the
archetype and its inevitable conclusion.

Few descriptions or analyses concerning Cocteau's
theater lack the terms "mécanisme," "enchaînement,"
"destin," "fugue," "précision," or "construction
rigoureuse." Whatever the tone or the genre may be,
however the signs or sequences may be arranged, the
process that determines the course of the whole is
inflexible. Portions of *La Machine infernale* reappear
in *Les Parents terribles*, just as vaudeville techniques
shape *La Machine infernale*, and aspects of *Renaud et
Armide* can be interchanged with those of *L'Aigle
à deux têtes*. Yet in whatever context these fragments
appear, they must continue to their predetermined end,
to the outcome that has somehow been "written."

That Cocteau sensed the machine-like characteristics of myth is further evidenced by early stage
experiments in which he adapted Greek tragedy almost without alteration. Considering the tempo of

Sophocles' era totally foreign to a twentieth-century audience, he condenses the dialogue in order that the major thrust and direction of the action will stand out. What dominates in each production is a rush to the end, an emphasis on the unavoidable outcome. Thus he underscores the fact that the drama's path has preexisted in its beginning, that nothing can deflect its course. For example, he characterizes *Antigone* as follows: "Le drame passe comme un express qui se hâte vers le déraillement final."[47] Such a treatment persists in each of his adaptations. He based *Le Pauvre matelot* on a situation that recurs frequently in folklore. A sailor has been away from his wife for many years. Having become wealthy, he returns disguised to his home, because he wants to see whether she has been faithful to him. He introduces himself as a wealthy friend of her husband and says that the latter will soon return. To obtain money for the homecoming, she kills him in his sleep. The motif appears to be a variation of the one from which Camus' *Le Malentendu* is derived; and Darius Milhaud, who wrote the score accompanying Cocteau's libretto, claims to have found it in a volume of Canadian legends.[48] Like *Antigone*, "le drame est traité en raccourci."[49] The repetitive, haunting quality of the music, patterned on folksongs and popular airs, reinforces an unswerving destiny and the reenactment of a story that cannot be changed.

If we accept the judgment that for Cocteau artistic motifs in general function much as do elements of a kaleidoscope and that the motifs he employed form the architectural shell of his work, it becomes evident that the construction of his plays reveals his perception

47. Cocteau, "A Propos d'*Antigone*," *Gazette des Sept Arts*, 10 December 1923.
48. Darius Milhaud, "*Le Pauvre matelot* et *Evolution*," *Paris-Soir*, December 9, 1929.
49. Ibid.

of the world: the threads that serve as components
of each work are analagous to components of a world-
machine. Cocteau's use of familiar motifs as structural devices rather than as vehicles for ideas distinguishes him from other modern playwrights and
underscores his emphasis on process over content. •

The second structural pattern from which Cocteau's
intuition of the real can be inferred is the play-within-
a-play which unites the concepts of the double and of
the mechanical. The works on which *Oedipe-Roi, La
Machine infernale, Antigone, Roméo et Juliette,* and
Phèdre are based apparently appealed to him because
of their essential duality. Where there was none—for
example, in the Orpheus legend—he added the strife
between Orpheus and the Bacchantes. The outcome
of each work depends not upon the seemingly major
plot line but on forces working outside the characters.
In *Oedipe-Roi* and *La Machine infernale*, for example,
the will of the gods or, in other words, the natural
processes in the universe rather than Oedipus himself
manipulate his life. Thus there is the play of the
hero's predicament and, encompassing it, the play of
the gods. Likewise, *Antigone* represents not only a
conflict between two kinds of authority but also the
presence of forces which make it inevitable that although Antigone dies, Creon is the one who even-
tually suffers more. *Roméo et Juliette* begins with a
confrontation between a Capulet and a Montagu;
within the framework of the two families' quarrel,
Romeo and Juliette's love develops and the couple
die. At every moment they are subject to the consequences of familial hatred: however reasonable he
attempts to be, for example, Romeo must kill Tybalt

because the latter mrdered his friend. Thus Romeo is
exiled. More important than the influence of the
Capulets and the Montagus, however, is what Frere
Laurent calls "un pouvoir mystérieux"[50] which
shapes the turn of events. *Phèdre* is not merely the
representation of unfortunate passion; it is, in addition, a manifestation of the curse on Hippolyte who
had insulted Aphrodite, and on the daughter of Minos
and Pasiphae. Renaud and Armide resemble Phèdre in
that they all play out a fate inherent to anyone who
possesses the fairies' ring: they are merely elements
in a play already written. To the Orpheus legend Cocteau added the relationship between Eurydice and the
Bacchantes, who, for no reason that appears to be
necessarily linked with the marriage, finally dismem-
ber the poet in the original myth. The playwright
thus combined the three salient facts known about
the hero—his vocation, his marriage, his death—and
suggested a latent scheme that connects them. In *Les
Monstres sacrés* and *Bacchus* major characters play
games while attempting to create a new reality within
a preexisting structure, and the tension of both plays
resides in a struggle between competing mechanisms.
Also, while trying to form her life into a work of art,
the Queen in *L'Aigle à deux têtes* appears to be
surrounded by forces that direct the course of events.
Les Parents terribles depicts yet another sort of
effort at freedom within a series of mechanisms that
cannot be altered.

However the universe may appear, however many
signs of free will or thought it may deceive man into
believing, within existence there is no accident, no
choice, certainly no chaos. It is true that the real

50. Cocteau,
Théâtre I, p.
114.

offers numerous possibilities of interpretation and that its surface is deceptive; nevertheless, reality exists as a coherent unit, unfolding according to certain laws. Each of Cocteau's plays contains incidents or occurrences that seem to have no reason or explanation. The camera in *Les Mariés* releases various animals or people instead of the customary bird. In *Roméo et Juliette* Romeo unknowingly falls in love with a girl whose family is the enemy of his own. Even when the two lovers think they have found a way to be united, there is a series of chance events that separate them: Romeo is exiled; Juliette is forced to marry Paris; each kills himself through a misunderstanding. Orpheus writes a poem that is an insult to contest judges; he accidentally looks at Eurydice when he knows that his glance will kill her. Michel in *Les Parents terribles* unwittingly falls in love with his father's mistress, as Oedipus did with his mother. Esther decides to introduce Liane into her home even though she realizes what the consequences may be. Renaud is mysteriously drawn to Armide's ring. The anarchist-poet who uses the pseudonym Azraël and looks exactly like the Queen's dead husband is chased into Kranz on the night of what would be the royal couple's tenth wedding anniversary; the Queen always keeps a vial of poison with her. Hans in *Bacchus* is elected to a position of absolute power over the village that has persecuted him. However aleatory each of these facts may appear to be in the context of the plot alone, they are all requisite components of the play and of the machine it imitates. Any alteration would change the work's development, and therefore what is chance from one

point of view becomes necessity from another. Every
play is both a machine and a disguise for a machine.
Even if the mechanism is hidden, it nevertheless
exists and cannot be understood until deciphered.
The plot of *La Machine infernale* is a game of the
gods which Oedipus and Jocasta do not understand
until they have been destroyed by it. The structural elements of *Renaud et Armide, Les Parents
terribles,* and *L'Aigle à deux têtes* resemble components that mechanically and inevitably produce a
result that could have been predicted if the forces at
work had been known. What is important is that the
forces are never evident; the characters in the play
occupy the same position in regard to their world as
the spectators do in regard to what is happening on
the stage. In each case so many factors are hidden
that the observer can grasp the truth only partially.
He is, therefore, a victim of illusion. Just as the
brooch and scarf in *La Machine infernale* mocked or
teased Jocasta, Orphée slowly repeats his horse's
message ("m-e-r-") and teases the public by shocking
it and tantalizing it at the same time. The third act
bedroom scene in *La Machine* plays on the same type
of ambivalence. Each word like each object and each
structure includes a sort of warning, a kind of indica-
tor that things are not what they seem. The complexity of the whole becomes evident only when the
mask (in whatever form it may take) is removed.

The relationship between appearance and reality in
Cocteau's world emerges as totally dialectical, since
nature generates signs (or appearance) that human
beings interpret, and these interpretations in turn
merge with the original givens to form something

51. Cocteau,
*L'Impromptu du
Palais-Royal*
(Paris: Galli-
mard, 1962),
pp. 7-8.

that is no longer pure objectivity. The real, therefore,
is always in process, always becoming rather than
being: an amalgamation of data in nature, of games,
of imagination, of subjective associations. Cocteau
never denied the existence of phenomena outside the
mind, but all facets of his work imply that he considered these phenomena as only a fragment of
reality: the real as a whole simply cannot exist without taking consciousness and perception into account.
A statement in *L'Impromptu du Palais-Royal* goes far
in revealing the poet's mental structures:

*Je projetais de marier, sans la moindre prudence, les
acteurs et les personnages qu'ils incarnent, d'en
faire un seul mélange, comparable aux contes de
Selma Lagerlöf, de Lewis Carroll et aux fables de la
Fontaine, ou les animaux parlent le langage des
hommes. Car c'est avec tendresse que Moliere dé-
clare: 'Ah! les étranges animaux à conduire que les
comédiens.'*[51]

By mentioning the names of Selma Lagerlöf and
Lewis Carroll, Cocteau immediately placed his last
work for the stage in a fantastic tradition that has
little if any relation to serious, logical works of art.
More important, however, in a light-hearted way his
very manner of expression represents an attack on
any kind of unidimensional stance vis-à-vis the world.
After describing a universe where animals can speak
the same language as human beings, he employed the
word "car" (i.e., a word that explains, that reveals
reasons) to connect his two uses of "animaux," uses

which in fact have no link other than an associational
one growing out of a play on words. Such a procedure
succinctly highlights the ricochets and leaps from
one level of meaning to another that characterize
his work as a whole. It is evident that Cocteau must
advance obliquely—in other words, completely on the
level of the *signifiant*—since he appears to deny if not
the existence of the *signifié*, at least its status as
something more than primarily subjective. For this
reason, the development of many of his early works
relies greatly on *signifiants* as generators of the action.
The course of *Les Mariés* and of *Orphée* depends as
much on the paths opened by linguistic possibilities
(i.e., the ambiguity of the word "balles") as it does
on any intellectualized, preconceived plot. The
duality inherent in many words and expressions permits a type of creation which, growing primarily out
of the *signifiant* (as most of Cocteau's poetry does),
underscores the instability of a real lacking an essence.
Likewise, on another level, instead of meaning something, his works function as *machines à signification*,
generators of meaning for each individual who comes
into contact with them.

Wherever we turn in Cocteau's work, the image of a
boîte à malices recurs in a mechanical way as well as
a deceptive context: machine-like functioning and
unstable configurations of signs comprise the basic
structures of his reality. Had Cocteau simply analyzed
and mastered his data by giving them an intellectual
order, his opus would have been different because, in
the final analysis, his relationship with the real as he
perceived (or intuited) it determined his relationship

with art. In the next chapter we will examine Cocteau's stance vis-à-vis the world and delineate the
esthetic that resulted from it.

3. The Nature of Art

In spite of the many directions they seem to take,
Cocteau's theoretical and critical works ultimately
revolve around preoccupations with illusion and fate.
For example, the nature of time (which implies
tempo as well as chronology) was a problem about
which Cocteau frequently wrote. Obviously, he had
no scientific training, but he nevertheless reacted to
(as opposed to analyzed) what he had heard about
Einstein's theory of relativity. It caught his attention
that time can be measured only in relation to movement of the observer rather than according to an
absolute, and therefore instead of time passing, the
individual passes through time. For reasons never
explained, Cocteau assumed the first three dimensions
to be a unit in which an infinite number of events had
been completed and ordered and which somehow
preexisted the fourth dimension (time). Time thus became the medium which allowed man to unroll
these happenings and to perceive intervals between
them. Within such a system, free will could be only
an illusion, since each person merely effects predetermined situations, the course of which he cannot
influence and about which he has no choice. Likewise,
Cocteau's reaction to certain documentaries in which

plant processes had been filmed and then shown at an
accelerated pace was that the validity of perception is
severely restricted, and his comments on dreams
reflect a great sensitivity to the unknown as well as
to the limitations of ordinary states of consciousness.

At certain key points, some of the elements of Cocteau's art coincide at least superficially with those
adopted by the Surrealists or Apollinaire: dreams and
the subconscious betoken an extension of the real;
conscious perception distorts reality by imposing
limited frameworks upon it; whole areas of the unknown remain to be explored with the tools offered
by Freud and Einstein; the age of speed and of complex machinery opens entirely new dimensions of the
merveilleux. For the surrealists, art functioned as a
liberating force, both socially and politically: like
Rimbaud, Breton believed that life would some day
be better if poets explored every aspect of existence,
if they went as far as possible toward grasping all a
human being could know. What separated Cocteau
(and consequently his art) from the groups with
which he came into contact was his intuition that
total knowledge led not to some joyous liberation but
to a sort of abyss, an awareness that no ultimate
meaning which gives stability to life exists. Whereas
for the surrealists art represented in part a kind of
questioning, for Cocteau it stood as a response; it
constituted his answer to a journey already taken:

*L'homme qui joue au jeu de l'art se mêle de ce qui le
regarde avec le risque d'ouvrir une brèche sur ce qui
ne la regarde pas. Les découvertes d'un Einstein
dépassent notre petite taille et n'arrivent pas aux*

pieds de Dieu. Il s'épuise dans le vide.[1]

As Jean Genet described his creations:

d'Opéra à Renaud et Armide, ces colonnes et temples cassés, nous les devinons être la forme visible d'une douleur et d'un désespoir qui choisirent de se dissimuler . . . Toute l'oeuvre craquèle et par les fissures laisse découvrir l'angoisse.[2]

Attempting to elucidate Cocteau by examining him within a tradition becomes helpful only if the critic follows Cocteau's own advice: "Il faut toujours en revenir à Nietzsche."[3] As was the case with Einstein, Eddington, Freud or any of the other thinkers about whom he wrote, the important issue becomes not so much whether he really understood Nietzsche or whether he had read everything the German had written, but rather, what aspects of Nietzsche's opus corresponded to his needs. If we view the German philosopher as trying to come to terms with a universe without God, with a world in which values depend on the subjectivity of human beings instead of on divine givens, then two distinct currents emerge. There was the strong Nietzsche, the Nietzsche who dominated a whole generation of such French intellectuals as Sartre, Malraux, Camus, and Gide with his analysis of the superman. The latter can joyously create his own values and therefore become a god by filling *le néant* with his will. The superman's nature is to overcome, to progress, to force mankind toward higher forms of consciousness and knowledge. On the other hand, however, there was the Nietzsche whose

1. Cocteau, *Le Rappel à l'ordre* (Paris: Stock, 1948), p. 224.
2. Jean Genet, "Jean Cocteau," *Empreintes*, May-June-July, 1950, pp. 23-24.
3. Jean Cocteau and André Fraigneau, *Entretiens avec André Fraigneau* (Paris: Union Générale d'Éditions, 1965), p. 2.

reaction to non-meaning lay in a desire to escape
lucidity, to flee the rational and lose all sense of self
in a communal, ritualistic frenzy; a Nietzsche who
questioned the value of thought and who postulated
that ultimate wisdom might reside in knowing how to
remain at the surface of things and how not to ask
questions; a Nietzsche for whom art's supremacy and
power resulted from the capacity of theater and
music to free spectators from anguish as it returned
them to a state of pre-conscious joy. The Nietzsche
whom Cocteau chose to eulogize was the latter, the
thinker of *The Birth of Tragedy, The Gay Science,*
and *The Case Wagner,* for example. Cocteau identified himself with these aspects of the German philosopher's thought because, as an examination of his
esthetic will reveal, he used art as a weapon against
illusion and fate, as a means of controlling the real.

Cocteau devoted a great part of his critical writing
to discussing his conception of the poet and of art in
general. As we saw when we deduced existential
premises from the structure of his work, what characterized his world view was a sense of fragmentation
and incoherence. His definition of the poet and his
description of art itself reflect the threads of the
double, codes, and the machine upon which his perception of the world was based.

Cocteau used the terms "poet" and "artist" as
synonyms: both mean "creator" regardless of the
artistic medium employed. Although he insisted that
each artist was unique, several traits they all appear
to share nevertheless stand out. First, each one is a
voyant in the Rimbaldian sense. He has suffered
greatly and journeyed so far toward what it is possible

for man to know that he has overstepped human
boundaries and has fallen from the paradisiacal state
of bliss that existed before knowledge of the human
condition: "Rimbaud, Mallarmé sont devenus Adam
et Eve, la pomme est de Cézanne. Nous porterons
toujours le poids du péché originel."[4] Second, he is a
fragmented individual belonging wholly to no one
sphere and striving to reconcile his contradictory
desires and characteristics. Third, because he has refused to suppress any part of himself, the seeds of all
human experience remain intact within him, and
through his search for form, for integration, they
emerge as art: "Nous pensons des formes, elles
deviennent vivantes sur le papier ou sur la toile sans
avoir aucun rapport avec les forces de la vie. Etre
sensible à la vérité des formes, c'est comprendre
l'art."[5]

It seems that in Cocteau's opinion the characteristic
that ultimately defines a poet is his possessing knowledge that average men lack. The creator exists *a
priori* as a superior being because he has probed
deeply in order to understand the secrets about himself and about the universe. Not satisfied with conventional explanations limited to what one perceives
through logic and the senses, he always reaches beyond the illusory and the mundane: having determined the narrow power of reason, he finds himself
no longer constrained by it and thus he can explore
more deeply than the philosopher and the scientist.

Although he has extraordinary gifts, the poet lives
in essence under a curse, because Cocteau implies that
the very knowledge which makes him an artist makes
him a divided human being; he suffers not only

4. Cocteau, *Rappel à l'ordre*, p. 183, note 1.
5. Cocteau, *Essai de critique indirecte* (Paris: Grasset, 1932), p. 108.

6. Cocteau,
"Poésie, arme
secrete,"
*Figaro littér-
aire*, June 23,
1956, p. 1.
7. Jean Cocteau
and Maurice
Rouzard, *En-
trevue sur la
critique* (Abbe-
ville: Impri-
merie F. Pail-
lard, 1929), p.
38.
8. Cocteau,
*Poésie criti-
que II* (Paris:
Gallimard,
1960), pp.
210-211.
9. Cocteau,
*Journal d'un
inconnu* (Paris:
Grasset, 1953),
p. 15.

because he desires to know more but, at the same
time, because he wants to flee from what he has experienced: "le poète se partage entre la peur d'affron-
ter le monstre et la dévorante curiosité de l'aper-
cevoir."[6] No longer able to exist comfortably within
any framework, he finds himself alienated from the
world at all levels as well as from himself: he is "un
amas de contradictions inconciliables."[7] He deliberately refuses conformity both to society and to any
accepted mode of perception since, were he to seek
happiness by giving up any of the numerous, conflicting facets of himself, he would consequently
sacrifice his being as a poet. Therefore, his very
nature resides in a kind of unhappy but resolute
balancing of opposites and in a refusal of compromise
that affronts and disturbs those around him.

In Cocteau's vocabulary, the artist's preservation of
all that constitutes him as an individual is called
maintaining his "line." Whereas most people capitulate to the norms of their time and civilization, he
remains unclassifiable and free, a sort of primeval
creature: "Le poète? Il n'est autre que la main-
d'oeuvre du schizophrène que chacun de nous porte
en soi et dont il est le seul à ne pas avoir honte."[8]
Hence, *une morale* becomes "un comportement
secret, une discipline construite selon les aptitudes
d'un homme refusant d'impératif catégorique, impératif qui fausse des mécanismes,"[9] and "purity"
means remaining uncorrupted by conformity, by
integration into the normal, unthinking ways of
seeing the universe. As a result, all threads of racial
memory, all elements of whatever heritage has been
deposited from generation to generation in the

human unconscious continue intact within him.

The poet's role in creation is double. On the one hand, the creator functions as a passive instrument through which unrefined and unadulterated forces pass. These forces have their origins in the subconscious or the "nuit," in Cocteau's vocabulary. At the same time, their roots extend to the sources of all human experience, since the artist acts as a repository for primeval urges, whether beneficial or destructive. Hence, the matter or stuff of art becomes the natural energy and pulsations of noncivilized life which Cocteau terms "poésie dans l'état brut."[10] When he speaks of the creator's work as changing his "night" into "day," he means that each artistic act results from the dark forces within the poet. On the other hand, "poésie à l'état brut" is not yet "poésie": "La seule excuse de l'artiste est d'apprivoiser la folie sous la forme transcendante du génie."[11] The work pre-exists, so to speak, in the artist; it manifests itself as a product of what Cocteau called "expiration" instead of "inspiration"; but in the final analysis the giving of form to what had been formless (and, hence, the creation of an art object) depends ultimately on a conscious self, on a state of awareness that deliberately shapes and controls raw material. The genesis of the art object consequently resembles the dialectical structure of reality itself: as we saw in Chapter 2 the real for Cocteau was apparently composed of an amalgamation of facts in nature with interpretations of these facts by a consciousness. Likewise, art results from the interplay or the meshing of primeval, untamed givens and the creator's will which shapes them.

10. Cocteau, *Rappel à l'ordre,* p. 218.
11. Cocteau, *Poésie critique II*, p. 211.

12. Cocteau,
Opium (Paris:
Stock, 1930),
p. 116.
13. Cocteau,
Rappel à l'ordre,
p. 218.

In such a context it is not surprising that the two
analogies that Cocteau most frequently employed in
describing the artist are those of the poet as child and
of the poet as tightrope walker. Children represent
an undisturbed, united self that existed before the
poet's journey toward knowledge; they are essentially
pre-adamic. Most important, not having assimilated
adult conceptions of the world, they exist completely
in harmony with their environment, and they compose such an integral part of it that they can control
it almost at will. There is no split between forces
suppressed within them and their social mask; they
have no need to be double. Therefore, they participate in a universe where artistic creation is a natural
function of existence, where games and the real inter-
mingle naturally to such an extent that distinguishing
them becomes impossible: "Tous les enfants ont un
pouvoir féerique de se changer en ce qu'ils veulent.
Les poètes en qui l'enfance se prolonge souffrent
beaucoup de perdre ce pouvoir."[12]

In his struggle to overcome fragmentation, Cocteau's poet always idealizes and seeks to regain his
childhood state: he is old and young at the same time.
He retains a child's creative potential, but he has
acquired the wisdom of old age. By this virtue of
balancing opposites, he resembles a tightrope artist.
Equilibrium represents a necessary condition for his
remaining a poet, because without it he has no choice
but to capitulate either to suicide or to conformity.
Since Cocteau defined poets as totally individualistic beings, and since he described art in terms of the
undeveloped poetry within each artist as "l'exercice
plus ou moins heureux par quoi on le domestique,"[13]

he viewed the history of art as a series of contradictions and revolutions: "Un chef-d'oeuvre, c'est
quelque chose qui dérange tout, qui ne ressemble à
rien . . . et qui change les règles du jeu."[14] He characterized each masterpiece's pattern of existence as an
initially shocking newness gradually assimilated into
the commonplace which is followed by another
revolt. Unlike science, however, that also evolves
through discoveries which alter its course, the history of art reflects no progess in the sense of ap-
proaching a goal, no logical connection between one
stage and the next. It is not possible to say that any
masterpiece is better than another; one can only say
that it is the apex of its genre or, if it is so nearly
unique as to be unclassifiable, that it is, simply,
beautiful. Moreover, since in his eyes, beauty results
from a revolt against what is currently accepted, and
because "l'esprit de création . . . est . . . la plus haute
forme de l'esprit de contradiction,"[15] Cocteau
condemns redoing what has already been done: "Ne
faites pas de l'art d'après l'art."[16]

Believing that the entire group of works rather than
a single opus reflected the complexity of each artist,
he maintained that such an esthetic of revolution
should apply not only to succeeding poets but also
to each creation of the same person:

Je ne pense pas qu'on progresse en se copiant et
j'estime qu'à cogner sur le même clou on finit par
l'aplatir. Une oeuvre ne vaut que si elle s'intègre
dans un oeuvre. C'est l'ensemble qui compte et la
répétition d'un style provoquerait cet ennui qu'on
respecte et que les lecteurs prennent pour une

14. Cocteau,
*Entretien avec
Roger Stéphane*
(Paris: R.T.F. et
la Librairie Jules
Tallandier, 1964),
p. 18.
15. Cocteau/
Rouzard, *Entre-
vue sur la critique*,
p. 19.
16. Cocteau,
Rappel à l'ordre,
p. 40.

17. Cocteau, *Le Cordon ombilical* (Paris: Plon, 1962), p. 15.
18. Quoted in Frederic Lefevre, *Une Heure avec . . .* (Paris: Editions de la Nouvelle Revue Française, 1924), p. 110.
19. Cocteau, *Essai de critique indirecte*, p. 43.

fidélité à soi-même, alors qu'il ne résulte que d'une paresse.[17]

Cocteau thus deliberately followed such a precept in his own work: "à chaque nouvel ouvrage, je tourne systématiquement le dos à l'ouvrage qui précède."[18] One reason for this attitude seems to be his conviction that modes of expression are almost unlimited: "La poésie s'exprime comme elle peut. Je lui refuse des limites."[19] Second, the many forces within him could not be exteriorized through a single genre or style; his own *morale*, his stance before existence, was too intricate to take form in a sole creative work. He needed a complex whole that could reflect the diverse facets of his perception. Third, since he was preoccupied with appearance and with how it can be manipulated, he was acutely aware that his work would be the only thing left of him after his death. Though he had no illusions about prevailing over critical interpretations that would follow his lifetime, he realized he could not be judged on what he had not produced. What an artist is can be made known only by his capturing aspects of himself in his poetry: he himself as a complete work cannot exist in history until this is done. If he leaves a great portion of himself hidden or unexpressed, then that part dies with him and never has the possibility of being understood. The living artist's imitating what he or someone else has already created is the equivalent of death: nothing new has come into existence to be recorded about him. It is as if he has already formed a part of history, of a past which he cannot alter, of a block of time in which everything to be done is completed:

"A notre mort, nos recherches cessent d'être des recherches; elles deviennent notre oeuvre."[20] A fourth reason can be found in Cocteau's attempt at *divertissement*, because movement itself became very important to him: "J'ai toujours préféré le mouvement aux écoles qui obligent un jour à s'asseoir."[21] Novelty obviously seemed a means of constant renewal, of returning to the beginning: "C'est le moyen de débuter toujours, donc de rester jeune."[22] Change represented, moreover, a way of suspending thought about himself, of being released from the power of reason which, through what it brings to light, makes action impossible; as he expressed it in a direct imitation of Nietzsche: "je ne pense pas, donc je suis. En somme, c'est ça le génie. La pensée retarde les actes."[23]

As we move from Cocteau's ideas on the poet to what he expected from art itself, the importance of *équilibre, divertissement,* illusion, machinery, and codes takes on an even greater dimension. The best introductions by Cocteau himself to the nature of art and the works which most clearly highlight the interdependence in his esthetic between creation and the real are his article "Le Numéro Barbette" (1926) and his last play, *L'Impromptu du Palais Royal* (1962). Although the article and the play appeared almost forty years apart, their unmistakable continuity underscores the fact that while superficially Cocteau's attitude toward art may appear contradictory, his basic stance did not change during his career.

"Barbette" (the stage name of Vander Clyde) was one of the most highly respected trapeze artists and female impersonators of the 1920's and 30's. Born in

20. Lefevre, p. 110.
21. Quoted in Christine Garnier, *L'Homme et son personnage* (Paris: Grasset, 1955), p. 65.
22. Lefevre, p. 110.
23. Quoted in Denise Bourdet, "Images de Paris," *La Revue de Paris,* 66 (May 1959), p. 136.

24. Cocteau,
"Le Numero
Barbette,"
*Nouvelle Revue
Française,* 27
(1926), p. 35.
25. Cocteau,
"Le Numero
Barbette," p.
36.

Texas, he performed in music halls and circuses
throughout Europe, although Paris—where he appeared at the Alhambra, the Casino de Paris, the
Moulin Rouge, the Empire, and the Médrano Circus—
remained his favorite city. It was in the French capital that Cocteau met him, saw his act, and became
intrigued by what he considered an outstanding example of theater craftsmanship. There is no doubt
that Cocteau's attraction to Barbette's performance
was largely sexual: the transvestite appeal of the act
can hardly be overlooked. Cocteau writes, for example, that "Barbette devient la femme-type au point
d'éteindre les plus jolies personnes qui le précèdent
et le suivent sur l'affiche."[24] Moreover, Barbette made
him understand why "les grands pays et les grandes
civilisations ne confiaient pas seulement par décence
les rôles de femmes à des hommes . . ."[25] However, the
subject matter of "Le Numéro Barbette" is ultimately
theoretical and based on the question of how codes
develop in a framework of ambiguous structures.

The strength and interest of Vander Clyde's act lay
in the fact that it was composed of (and could not
exist without) two skills: the performer had to be not
only a female impersonator but also an accomplished
acrobat. When Barbette came on stage, he was dressed
as a woman. To allay any suspicions the audience
might have, he performed a kind of strip tease until
he was wearing only a female acrobat's costume. In
this way he pantomimed a fairly erotic scene which
established his sex. Yet since Barbette was presented
to the spectators as a tightrope artist, this sequence
was actually only a beginning. As Cocteau remarks,
"il jette sa poudre aux yeux. Il la jette d'un coup,

d'une telle poigne, qui'il va pouvoir se permettre de
ne plus penser qu'au travail d'équilibriste . . ."[26] At
the end of the act he was applauded for his tightrope
performance, and Cocteau was not the only reviewer
to note the many curtain calls he received. Hence,
he was an excellent acrobatic artist, enthusiastically
praised for that talent alone. It was only after such a
response that he took off his wig. From accounts of
audience reaction, it seems clear that most people
were taken completely by surprise. Cocteau describes
the wave of astonishment in the room and many em-
barrassed, disbelieving faces. Just as Barbette had
introduced his act by miming the essence of feminin-
ity, he ended it by playing an extremely masculine role.
According to Cocteau, his simply being a man was
not sufficient in the circumstances. Therefore, he had
to continue performing, he had to exaggerate: he
flexed his muscles and hopped from one foot to the
other, resembling a mischievous street urchin.

Were it not for the virtual impossibility of success
in what Barbette attempted, his performance would
be of little interest. Miraculously, he was able to con-
vince large numbers of spectators to accept him as a
female acrobat. He did not imitate a woman in order
that his audience immediately perceive his imitation
and react to it as a facet of his art. Rather, for them,
his sex in theory was not even supposed to come into
question. Yet Vander Clyde was a trapeze artist.
With each motion, his body or his costume should
have betrayed him, since nothing he did on stage was
passive. Obviously, then, he had learned to suppress
all types of movement natural to a man, he had
scrutinized each step of his routine and eliminated

26. Ibid.

27. Ibid., p. 35.

everything masculine. Such an attempt would be
difficult enough in nondemanding activities like
walking, but in strenuous acrobatics even reflex
actions would have to be controlled to an almost
unattainable extent. Moreover, his brief costume
made the task all the more difficult. The two aspects
of Barbette's act that distinguish it from all others resembling it are its premise of total illusion or deception and its impeccable craftsmanship. These are
precisely the two subjects that form the core of Cocteau's article.

*Car n'oubliez pas, nous sommes dans cette lumière
magique du théâtre, dans cette boîte à malices où
le vrai n'a plus cours, où le naturel n'a plus aucune
valeur, où les petites tailles s'allongent, les hautes
statures rapétissent, où des tours de cartes et de
passe-passe, dont le public ne soupconne pas la
difficulté, parviennent seuls à tenir le coup.*[27]

It is clear that for Cocteau entering an auditorium
was tantamount to participating in a reality completely
removed from that of every day. Different rules apply
and, most important, the nature of perception
changes completely. If the theater has a "magic light"
that distorts ordinary objects, then whatever is presented on the stage must first be altered: it must be
transposed just as music is transposed from key to
key. In most cases actors realize such a transforma-
tion through their make-up or costumes. Yet they
usually retain elements of who they really are, whereas Barbette succeeded in altering who he was as completely as possible.

The basic assumption underlying Cocteau's conception of art as presented in "le Numéro Barbette,"—an assumption that is a mirror image of his relationship with the real—is his tenet that creation presupposes deception: obviously, the words "malice box," "sleight of hand," and "card tricks" come to mind. Art is a game whose success depends on the degree to which the audience accepts the game as reality. While modifications of such a position are not uncommon in the history of theater, Cocteau's stand is extreme in that it contains such great emphasis on shifting from one type of reality to another. That Vander Clyde was a great acrobat would not have intrigued Cocteau, although he certainly would not have underestimated the skill involved. Rather, his ability to portray a female trapeze artist supplied the trick, the "sleight of hand," necessary to raise his performance to the status of genuine theater. For art to exist, the simple convention of illusion that underlies most acting is not enough; there must be a double order of illusion, a double step from commonplace reality: the female impersonator Vander Clyde exists behind the trapeze artist Barbette.

Without a doubt, the work that in conjunction with "Le Numéro Barbette" best illustrates Cocteau's esthetic is *L'Impromptu du Palais Royal*. Though it seems more complex because it is in the form of a play with dialogue, it is nevertheless—with the exception of a discussion on the nature of time—little more than a statement of the concepts that can be deduced from Cocteau's article. As its title indicates, it falls into the category of plays like Molière's *Impromptu de Versailles* and *La Critique de L'Ecole des femmes*

or Giraudoux's *Impromptu de Paris*, in which the subject of the work is theater. Both Molière and Giraudoux wrote scripts in which the characters consisted
of a troupe of actors supposedly at ease and speaking
informally. Obviously, such a device is a convention,
but it is one that intrigued Cocteau because of its
essential ambiguity: in an impromptu actors appear
not to be acting. They are therefore playing the role
of actors, and the action merely seems to be unprac-
ticed. Consequently, such a form presented an ideal
vehicle for the expression of ideas on illusion, tricks,
and machine-like perfection.

Cocteau wrote *L'Impromptu du Palais Royal* as a
prologue and divertissement for the *Fourberies de
Scapin*, which the Comédie Française presented on a
tour to Japan. Using the general pretext of rehearsal
for a Molière play, he complicated his sketch by
making it a sort of impromptu within an impromptu,
just as Barbette's act is a performance within a performance. In Giraudoux's *Impromptu de Paris*, for
example, the cast was composed of Jouvet and his
company at the Athénée, and although the "rehearsal" begins with a few lines from Molière's *Impromptu* to set the tone for what is to follow, the
actors nevertheless represent only members of the
twentieth-century troup. Cocteau, however, con-
fused matters by a twofold departure from the spectator's world: his actors play the role not merely of
actors but of actors who on a bare stage are in the
process of improvising a sketch about Molière, Louis
XIV, and the court while they wait for the "real"
Molière play to begin. Being about theater, the work
is consequently about game, and it depicts a cast

"playing" before it starts to work. Therefore, many of Cocteau's own ideas are expressed by such characters as the King, Monsieur, or Molière himself, and there is a constant juxtaposition of the production's two levels as the actors slip naturally in and out of their improvisation. At each turn the spectacle is a conjunction of truth and illusion. The audience is always aware that what happens at the court of Louis XIV is determined by actors who are improvising, that in fact every word or gesture was selected by the author. By unmasking dramatic conventions, Cocteau destroys the myth of spontaneity and allows his spectators to glimpse the secrets of dramatic art. However, he does so in such a charming, indirect fashion that the *Impromptu* is probably one of his greatest triumphs in sleight of hand.

At the beginning, in a sort of prologue, a man putting on a marquis' costume as he enters stops to speak to the public as if he were addressing it casually. However, he breaks down one level of illusion by explaining that he is really not a marquis but an actor and that in spite of the freedom Cocteau has left the cast, the essence of the improvisation the spectators are about to see is "un épouvantable mélange de ce que nous sommes et de ce que nous ne sommes pas. Un piège! . . . Ne vous y trompez pas. Les extravagances que vous allez entendre sont bel et bien de sa plume et nous les avons apprises."[28] While he is speaking, a lady in the audience interrupts to correct his pronounciation. She is usually a member of the troupe, she claims, but now she is a spectator and she is going to use the liberty the author has given her by stopping the action and expressing her opinions. Yet,

28. Cocteau, "Arthur Rimbaud," *Aujourd'hui*, March 24, 1941.

29. Guillaume
Apollinaire,
"L'Esprit nouveau
et les poètes,"
*Mercure de
France*, 1
décembre 1918,
p. 393.
30. Cocteau,
*Mon premier
voyage* (Paris:
Gallimard,
1936), p. 184.
31. Cocteau,
Journal, p. 160.

it is obvious that her freedom is only a fiction, that
everything she says is in fact a part of a carefully
worded script. Likewise, the Marquise explains to the
Duke that "nous jouons ici double jeu . . . Dansez,
Messieurs . . . Dansez au bout des fils que l'auteur
invisible anime au-dessus de nous."[29] Molière, who is
frequently Cocteau's spokesman, states that "notre
métier consiste à confondre le vrai et le faux."[30]
Often the actors argue among themselves about an
interpretation of their roles in such a fashion that the
elements of game or play which underlie the whole
production become evident through their badinage.
They make direct allusion to their improvisation
while they correct each other's mistakes. The tone is
light throughout as members of the troupe follow
remarks about Molière with comments on Cocteau,
and as they mingle the two levels of action. "Saint-
Simon" for example is waiting for a propitious moment when he can introduce his actress girl friend to
the King. At one of the King's statements, the "spectator" bursts out with: "Ça, c'est du Cocteau cent
pour cent et jamais le Roi Louis XIV ne se serait avisé
d'avoir une idée pareille."[31] Moreover, at the end of
the script Cocteau indicates that if there are curtain
calls, the cast should come out to bow in whatever
they happen to have on, whether it be street clothes
or costumes for the play following *L'Impromptu*. The
atmosphere created by the work is one of effortless-
ness, informality, and gaiety. The spectator certainly
does not leave the auditiorium with an impression
of having heard a treatise on theater, because the
machinery of the production is carefully hidden and
calculated to function only indirectly.

However many years may separate Barbette's act from *L'Impromptu du Palais Royal*, the formal continuity between the two works is nevertheless unmistakable. To qualify as art, a performance must surpass the old truism of "realistic representation." The reality of poetry has as its very basis the concept of trickery—and not merely a shoddy make-believe, but a game so convincingly and skillfully formed as to be accepted on its own terms. The artist's world should charm the spectator, captivate him so that he falls under its spell. Representation is not sufficient: what is presented must be perceived without question as what it purports to be.

The secret behind achieving such a goal appears to be a well-constructed machine, in Cocteau's vocabulary. No detail is left to chance. Even in the *Impromptu*, whose characters blatantly inform the spectator at every turn that he is being deceived, the cleverness of the dialogue creates an impression of improvisation. The structure of the replies is such that the two planes of game interact in quick ricochets which evoke carefree play. Paradoxically, making a series of actions look unplanned requires the utmost in preparation. Each component of the whole must be properly timed, properly arranged. Underlying every successful work for the stage, Cocteau would argue, whether on the level of choreography, performance, or text, is a guiding mechanism that denies the premise of chance in art.

In the light of "Le Numéro Barbette," *L'Impromptu du Palais Royal*, and the mass of Cocteau's critical writings, several assumptions concerning art, its relationship with the real, and its influence on the

32. Quoted in
A.R., "Le Poéte
vit dans un
rêve . . ."
*Résistance-Paris
Matin*, Decem-
ber 21, 1946.

public emerge clearly. In the first place, Cocteau
demanded that art represent the real—not that it imitate details, but that it capture basic structures or
configurations. At the same time, having described
the journey toward understanding reality as a journey
toward "le vide," he then demanded that the work of
art somehow hide the truth, that it be constructed in
"chiffres" or "hiéroglyphes" which would have to be
deciphered before they could be fully understood. In
this way, perhaps without realizing it, he established
two distinct tiers of public reaction or appreciation.
He spoke very little about one of these and in fact
mentioned it only in terms of his own creation. After
his death, he claimed, when his work would be complete, a careful observer could examine the whole and
determine the structures that compose it:

> *toute mon oeuvre . . . est un phénomène de perspec-
> tive. Elle ressemble à certains trompe-l'oeil des
> Hollandais. Je la mène de telle sorte qu'on ne puisse
> en voir le sens général que de loin, sous un certain
> éclairage: celui de la mort. De près, on distingue les
> éléments qui préparent cette visibilité posthume.
> Voila pourquoi j'excuse tant de critiques qui se
> trompent.*[32]

He thus defined the entirety of his art as an appropriate field for systematic analysis. Yet such a position is highly exceptional in his writing. The dominant
stance, rather, is that the work of art exists to appeal
to each human being's need for *évasion*: that at its
best, it should provide a sort of communal experience
which momentarily frees the individual from solitude

and from the burdens of his daily life. For Cocteau, in the final analysis, one of the most important indicators of a work's success lay in whether the public had been affected emotionally by having come into contact with it. Finally, he believed, the only kind of art object with the potential of touching the public was one assembled with a detailed, precise craftsmanship; or, as he said many times, with the precision of a perfect machine.

"Le poète vit dans le monde *réel*. On le redoute parce qu'il met le nez de l'homme dans sa crotte."[33] Since, according to Cocteau, only the poet was capable of grasping the real in its totality, and since the work of art was an emanation or an "expiration" (as opposed to "inspiration") from the artist, each art object necessarily reflected reality. Yet Cocteau never meant this in the traditional sense of the word "realism"—that is, in the sense of imitating details in nature. Reality for him implied form and structure rather than content; any other definition lacked substance: "La forme doit être la forme de l'esprit. Non pas la manière de dire les choses, mais de les penser."[34] Therefore, his esthetic position stood diametrically opposed to Antoine's or to Zola's, for example, since the naturalists evidently believed that the real could be quantitatively conveyed to the public, that its totality could be copied particle by particle, and that such an achievement could be termed "art." Because Cocteau's premises in regard to his surroundings were so different from theirs, his esthetic insofar as realism was concerned reflected an interaction between nature and consciousness which the naturalists did not take into account.

33. Cocteau, *Mon Premier Voyage*, p. 184.
34. Cocteau, *Rappel à l'ordre*, p. 230.

35. Cocteau, *La Difficulté d'être* (Paris: Union Générale d'Editions, 1957), p. 145.
36. Cocteau, "Secrets de la beauté," *Fontaine*, 42 (1945), p. 176.
37. Cocteau, "Zola le poéte," *Cahiers naturalistes*, 11 (1958), p. 442.
38. Cocteau/Fraigneau, *Entretiens avec André Fraigneau*, pp. 65–66.

Like Picasso or the surrealists, Cocteau viewed the relationship between art and the world in terms of the artist's orientation rather than in terms of some absolute. When he said that "l'art existe à la minute où l'artiste s'écarte de la nature,"[35] he placed art's domain in creation and in self-expression rather than in servile imitation. As in many esthetic movements of his period, for Cocteau value and interest resided in a portrait of the artist's perception instead of a perfect reproduction of the universe—an impossible task. With essence and meaning thrown into doubt, the stability as well as the communicating power of language in which Flaubert or Zola had apparently believed and on which they had predicated their art no longer held: "Ce n'est pas en écrivant le mot table que vous parlerez d'une table":[36] traditional techniques were insufficient to deal with a multidimensional real and its mirror-like structure. Cocteau apparently believed that each artist's point of view determined the real that was presented in his works and that no perspective could be called more nearly accurate than another. He therefore described realism as "peindre avec exactitude les objets d'un monde propre à l'artiste et sans le moindre rapport avec ce qu'on a coutume de prendre pour la réalité,"[37] and he avoided any claim to universal validity: "ces oeuvres ne sont réalistes que par rapport à nous."[38] The art object existed, then, as a concrete manifestation of the poet's mind or as a nonabstract embodiment of the union between "poésie brut" and the artist's consciousness—that is, as an exteriorization of his reality.

Within such a framework, it is not surprising that

his own goal in creation was the attainment of what
he called "le plus vrai que le vrai,"[39] an expression
introduced in his preface to *Les Mariés de la Tour
Eiffel*. The techniques he chose to use were inspired
by Picasso's presentation of ordinary objects in
unusual surroundings or in relationships which liber-
ated them from their expected functions in the world
and which implied that their existence had numerous
perspectives usually hidden to the observer because
of habit:

*L'espace d'un éclair, nous voyons un chien, un fiacre,
une maison pour la première fois. Tout ce qu'ils
présentent de spécial, de fou, de ridicule, de beau
nous accable. Immédiatement après, l'habitude frotte
cette image puissante avec sa gomme. Nous caressons
le chien, nous arrêtons le fiacre, nous habitons la
maison. Nous le les voyons plus.*[40]

One example of this would be the bull's head that
Picasso evoked by placing a bicycle's handlebars over
the seat: or, in Cocteau's words: "objets communs re-
connaissables mais transcendés, vus et déchiffrés dans
un autre contexte fastueux, tout en trahissant sans
cesse la pauvreté de leur origine, leur banalité."[41] In
a parallel example of this device (*Le Jeune homme et
la mort*) Cocteau altered everyday gestures or movements until they became dance movements, until
they attained an equilibrium between two levels of
reality, an equilibrium which sketched the portrait
of a reality and of a mind characterized by their
nature double.

Up to this point, Cocteau's esthetic offers nothing

39. Cocteau, *Théâtre I*, p. 4.
40. Cocteau, *Le Secret professionnel*, p. 215.
41. Jean-Marie Magnan, "La Machine à signi-fications," *La Revue de Paris*, 72 (December 1965), p. 52.

42. Cocteau,
*Essai de cri-
tique indirecte,*
p. 199.

really original: it clearly participates in the surrealist
and cubist spirit of breaking away from traditional
relationships between art and the real. Even as early
as *Le Coq et l'Harlequin*, Cocteau had toyed with the
ideas of contradiction and revolution, and the concept of a music fitting for twentieth-century expectations, with a new "battle of the ancients and the
moderns" that pitted the *Groupe des Six* against
Debussy and Fauré. Where Cocteau diverged from his
contemporaries was in his assertion that art not only
unveils many previously hidden aspects of the real
but, at the same time, hides, out of necessity, "une
des formes les plus gênantes de la vérité."[42] The
origins of the stance apparently lie in Cocteau's
reaction to the poet's journey toward knowledge,
which he saw as contradictory: though the artist had
access to realms denied to ordinary human beings,
though he could uncover beauty and free himself and
others from habit-found modes of perception, he
nevertheless ended his voyage in nothingness; he
found no God, no core of meaning; in the end, he
discovered only endless flux. Cocteau's art existed as
a kind of primitive chant or exhortation against this
void—not as an attempt to abolish it or to give it
meaning, but as an effort to make it bearable and to
best it whenever possible on its own terms. Like Barbette's performance or *L'Impromptu du Palais Royal*,
all of Cocteau's work was constructed to deceive and
to entertain. The methods of deception reflected
those built into the cosmos' functioning at the same
time that the entertaining aspects were calculated to
hide the void behind numerous doubles and disguises.
Cocteau's reaction to a statement made by one of

Tibet's Dali Lamas succinctly indicates his attitude: "'le secret du Thibet, c'est qu'il n'y en a pas et c'est celui qu'il faut protéger avant tout autre.' Ce mot admirable m'a profondément touché."[43] Such, it would appear, was Cocteau's own "secret," which he guarded: that there was no secret awaiting the artist when he finished his journey, and consequently that there was none in the work of art; instead of a message or a truth there was only emptiness. "J'ai masqué le drame du *Potomak* sous mille farces," he wrote. "Ainsi chante-t-on pour se donner du coeur dans le noir."[44] One of his criteria for significant art, then, was the presence of *chiffres* or *hiéroglyphes* which had to be deciphered if the work was to be understood.

The fragmentation evidenced by Cocteau's world view is directly mirrored in his esthetic by the tension between an art that reveals at the same time that it hides. Like the real and like the poet's nature, art manifests itself as an equilibrium, the coexistence of opposites, something which exhibits differing but equally valid characteristics depending on the perspective from which it is viewed.

In this light, only the structures inherent to theater—game, rite, play, ceremony—ultimately fulfilled the entire gamut of Cocteau's esthetic needs. In the first place, the notion of a stage and of actors— perfectly embodied in *L'Impromptu du Palais Royal* —reflected the dualism underlying his existential and esthetic positions:

j'ai souvent répété qu'une chose ne pouvait à la fois être et avoir l'air. Ce crédo perd de son exactitude

43. Quoted in Christine Garnier, *L'Homme et son personnage*, p. 67.
44. Cocteau, *Le Secret professionnel*, p. 227.

45. Cocteau,
Théâtre I,
p. 199.

*lorsqu'il s'agit du théâtre, sorte d'enchantement assez
louche où l'avoir l'air règne comme le trompe-l'oeil
sur les plafonds italiens.*[45]

Second, material presented on a stage can rarely be as
accessible to the intelligence as a written text, simply
because of time limitations; there is little opportunity
to review or analyze immediately something whose
movement cannot be stopped and reflected upon;
only later, either through memory or a script, will the
spectator have the opportunity to move beyond surface impression of his experience. Consequently,
since they take the form both of *spectacle* and book,
theater and related arts allow for a double sort of
interpretation: an emotional, intuitive one during the
performance, and, if desired by the spectator, a
further exploration of the text or choreography. In
this way, theater offered Cocteau a field with the
potential of revealing and hiding at the same time, of
entertaining his public with the glitter and cleverness
of his work while concealing its pessimism within
its structure. All his work, of whatever genre, followed this theatrical pattern of a surface virtuosity
coupled with a hidden portrait, a split between tone
and *fond* designed not for the sake of irony but for
divertissement and protection. Finally, for Cocteau,
the theatrical experience—and, by extension, all game
experiences (such as those portrayed in *Thomas
l'Imposteur* and *Les Enfants terribles*) as well as all
types of performance (such as poetry reading)—represented one level of defense provided by art against
emptiness. When he wrote about the stage, the
qualities to which he most frequently alluded were

its potential for establishing communication between
salle and *scene* through an "exchange of waves" or
a collective hypnosis; its capacity for freeing the
audience from the limitations of a habit-bound existence, even if only momentarily; and the possibilities
within it for enabling each spectator to recapture the
state of mind preceding that of the divided, lucid self,
a state which resembles childhood.

Cocteau defined the theater experience as "un rêve
extérieur partagé avec nous par le reste du public,"[46]
and he felt very strongly that what he called an "exchange of waves" must take place between the
audience and the action on the stage. He wanted to
create a private world and invite his public inside,
much as children fashion games to play with each
other. While the game continued, he hoped that it
would absorb its participants completely, that all
other reality would disappear and the world of the
artist's mind would for a while exist as the only real.
He once remarked, for example, that a poet's dream
was not to be famous but to be "believed," to create
a universe that might replace the usual one in which
human beings lived every day.

Such art provided an atmosphere in which a work
and its public might be united in a bond that made
communication possible through what Cocteau called
"collective hypnosis": the nature of the performance
encouraged each spectator to suspend his intellect
and react to what he saw as a young person might. He
believed that not only barriers between stage and
audience could be abolished, but each social or personal wall that ordinarily separated individuals could
be overcome:

46. Cocteau, *Foyer des artistes* (Paris: Plon, 1947), p. 154.

47. Cocteau, *La Difficulté d'être*, p. 167.
48. Cocteau, "Propos sur la culture," *La Nef*, no. 11 (December 1955), p. 208.

Une minute de contact entre une salle et une oeuvre supprime momentanément l'espace qui nous sépare d'autrui. Ce phénomène . . . nous permet de vivre dans un monde où le cérémonial de la politesse arrive seul à nous donner le change sur l'écoeurante solitude de l'être humain.[47]

He sought to create "un spectacle ayant pour but de désindividualiser les individus jusqu'à ce qu'ils ne forment plus qu'une seule personne enfantine et perméable."[48] As the participant abandons his habitual, adult mode of consciousness, he in a sense returns to a child's relationship with the world, in which the perceiver experiences *le merveilleux* for the first time. United into a single body with those around him, he loses awareness of himself as an individual and becomes a part of the work before him. For a short while, solitude and fragmentation cease, and life assumes the form it had before man's consciousness of *le néant*: a primeval bliss where play was a natural process and did not simply function as a ploy against emptiness. For Cocteau, as the following description by Pierre-Aimé Touchard indicates, theater is a sacred ceremony, a ritual central to life:

Un soir que j'étais allé voir Jean Cocteau au Théâtre Hébertôt pendant une représentation de L'Aigle à deux têtes, *il m'entraîna dans un couloir dont les portes donnaient sur la salle et me fit observer le public par une petite ouverture qui permettait de regarder sans être vu. Le silence était total, religieux, tous les visages tendus vers les comédiens dans une même expression d'intérêt passionné, de sympathie*

profonde. 'Pour moi, me dit Cocteau, les regarder
ainsi, c'est ma plus grande joie au théâtre.' Le vieux
poète était en effet particulièrement sensible à cette
étonnante magie du spectacle qui fait que des in-
connus rassemblés par hasard puissent s'unir dans un
sentiment de communion avec les personnages
fictifs, jusqu'à ne plus respirer que du même inten-
sité, les mêmes joies ou les mêmes souffrances.[49]

The key to creating a *spectacle* that resembled
envoûtement lay in perfect, machine-like craftsmanship: "la poésie en général . . . est une machine de
précision."[50] If each element, no matter how small,
had not been minutely planned, the work would fail
to provoke the ecstatic, almost sexual reaction which
alone permitted a spectator to enter into the ceremony. As was the case with Barbette's act, any detail
out of place destroyed the dream world and broke
the illusion so necessary to the kind of belief that
made an esthetic experience possible. For this reason,
mise en scène frequently dominated the script: each
kind of technique (aural as well as visual) had the
potential of appealing to a different sense or emotion,
and no single category of *éléments sceniques* was
supposed to dominate another.

In this context, the *monstre sacré* tradition on
which Cocteau often drew becomes very interesting,
as he has been accused of relying too heavily on
certain popular actors or actresses in order to create
successes and social triumphs. It would be foolish to
deny Cocteau's connection with the Tout-Paris and
with Parisian upper-middle class theater circles; but
one must remember that while Edwige Feuillère, Jean

49. Quoted in
Pierre-Aimé
Touchard, *Le
Théâtre et
l'angoisse des
hommes* (Paris:
Editions du
Seuil, 1964), p.
209.
50. Cocteau and
Pierre Lagarde,
"Interview sur
la poésie,"
Conférencia, 2
(1938), p. 539.

Marais, or Berthe Bovy were the idols of a certain
social set, they were at the same time almost perfect
instruments for the creation of *spectacle* or of
grandiose, romantic, compelling drama. They seem to
have appealed as much to the child in Cocteau as to
the snob, since only they were the type who could
make star-crossed lovers believable and who could
make the realm of myth and fairy tale come alive for
his public. These *vedettes* formed an integral part of
his *machine à envoûter*; he should not be condemned
for bad faith, then, when he states that actors serve
the poet rather than vice versa, or that an actress
cannot replace one gesture by another without upsetting the equilibrium of a work. Although Madame
Poposco's accent and *jeu* in *La Machine infernale*
probably represented a sort of pandering to the
audience, they also function as necessary cogs in the
dramatic machine.

Another ramification of the use Cocteau made of
dramatic machinery in all senses of the term (structural as well as spectacular) revolves around the problem of meaning in art. In the introductory notes of
almost every play, Cocteau carefully warned the
reader that he was not writing to explain the good
but rather to present as objectively as possible his perception of what is. It seems that if he had wanted to
take the side of a particular character or philosophy,
he would not have followed his models so closely; he
would have altered them in such a fashion that a
single position would have emerged as the right one.
Yet this is precisely what he does not do. For example, Neal Oxenhandler said of *Les Chevaliers*
that Cocteau in his preface "tries . . . openly . . . to

discount the triumph of Galaad, as if he were not altogether comfortable with it,"[51] and of *Les Parents terribles* that "a condemnatory attitude is definitely suggested"[52] toward the incestuous relationship between Yvonne and Michel. If he were a moralist, however, as Oxenhandler claims, he could very well have altered each action to suit his own purposes. He could have stated explicitly that Arthur's view is the correct one or, on the other hand, that Galaad is the hero-redeemer of all the characters. Instead, he retained an ambiguity that implied a world without absolute moral values: good and bad exist only in relation to an individual. In *Les Parents terribles*, he provided "un enchaînement logique de circonstances illogiques"[53] and followed his *données* to their logical conclusion: once the machine was set in motion, its components' traditional path determined its product. It seems that Cocteau reminded his public whenever he could that he did not write *pièces à thèse*, since like his Greek models and Nietzsche, he could not claim to have discovered reasons or meaning for anything: the world-machine simply goes on as it has eternally. Cocteau has frequently been criticized for this lack of position or of a moral stance, but his perceptual mode made such a response impossible, for his structure was his message and entertainment was the first stage of his existential response.

As we examine the definitions and relationships that characterize Cocteau's esthetic triad (poet, art object, public) and compare them with Nietzsche's premises in *The Birth of Tragedy*, the similarities between the two stand out clearly:

51. Neal Oxenhandler, *Scandal and Parade* (New Brunswick, N. J., Rutgers University Press, 1957), p. 191.
52. Ibid., p. 192.
53. Cocteau, *Théâtre I*, p. 424.

54. Friedrich
Nietzsche, *The
Birth of
Tragedy*, tr.
Walter Kauf-
mann (New
York: Vintage
Books, 1967),
pp. 60, 73.

*In this sense the Dionysian man resembles Ham-
let: both have once looked truly into the essence of
things, they have* gained knowledge, *and nausea
inhibits action; for their action could not change anything in the eternal nature of things; they feel it to be
ridiculous or humiliating that they should be asked to
get right a world that is out of joint. Knowledge kills
action; action requires the veils of illusion . . . true
knowledge, an insight in the horrible truth, out-
weighs any motive for action . . .*

*Now no comfort avails any more; longing tran-
scends a world after death, even the gods; existence
is negated along with its glittering reflection in the
gods or in an immortal beyond. Conscious of the
truth he has once seen, man now sees everywhere
only the horror or absurdity of existence . . .*

Here, when the danger to his will is greatest,
art *approaches as a saving sorceress, expert at healing.
She alone knows how to turn these nauseous
thoughts about the horror or absurdity of existence
into notions with which one can live . . .*

*. . . the hero is the suffering Dionysus of the Myster-
ies, the god experiencing in himself the agonies of
individuation, of whom wonderful myths tell that as
a boy he was torn to pieces by the Titans and now is
worshipped in this state as Zagreus. Thus it is inti-
mated that this dismemberment, the properly Dionysian suffering, is like a transformation into air, water,
earth, and fire, that we are therefore to regard the
state of individuation as the origin and primal cause
of all suffering, as something objectionable in itself.*[54]

Whether Cocteau was an intellectual, whether he had
read and assimilated the German philosopher's ideas,
he nevertheless encapsulates certain mental structures
implicit in Nietzsche's development. On many levels,
Cocteau created superficial art, but he did so deliberately. He may never have been able to express his
goals as theories, but he intuited that art represented
momentary salvation precisely because it could keep
the individual at the surface of himself—rather than
plunging a spectator into labyrinths that lead only
toward emptiness, a ritualistic, gamelike experience
liberates him from the consequences of intro-
spection. Cocteau was fascinated with dance, for
example, because it contained no words that might
appeal to the intellect and break the charm of the
performance; ballet's *envoûtement* grew out of
primitive frenzy having nothing to do with the mind.
Moreover, since they transcended barriers of nationality and time, the signs that constituted its language
reached a much wider audience and created a larger
community than ordinarily possible. What Nietzsche
saw in Greek art with its struggle between the Apol-
lonian and Dionysian was creation which owed its
existence to a synthesis of opposites and which had
developed to fill and to hide a lack: creation that
masked nothingness behind appearances. Nietzsche
had called for a gay, laughing art, and Cocteau believed that this was the kind of art he had produced.

4. The Role of Myth

During a performance or at a first reading, Cocteau's work often gives the impression of being merely entertaining or clever. The evident preoccupation with *métier* and craftsmanship lends even more credence to an evaluation of Cocteau as a skilled impresario but little else. Moreover, it is certain that he strove for a light, diverting art, that he would never have denied the importance of play in everything he created. Nevertheless, the question remains whether his art possesses more than a momentary liberating force and whether it contains wider implications than simple entertainment does. As we have indicated, Cocteau hinted that his work had significance beyond its value as *divertissement*, but to answer the question properly we must turn to mythology because, as Milorad has pointed out, Cocteau was a *mythographe* in two senses of the word: he created his own myths while building his work on those of many countries and many traditions. In one form or another, myth permeates everything he created, and it yields the only key to a mental set where art alone has ultimate power.

Few topics have received more attention in recent literary criticism than that of myth. The problem is

complicated by multitudinous and often conflicting
interpretations of what constitutes a myth, a mythic
theme, or a motif. For example, adaptations of
classical Greek tragedies are a recurring feature of
twentieth-century French theater. Gide, Sartre,
Giraudoux, and Anouilh in addition to Cocteau have
chosen to express their ideas in a framework provided
by Sophocles, Euripides, or Aeschylus, Yet, as Mircia
Eliade and others have pointed out, what we usually
call "myth" is an artistic form rather than a direct
religious expression; that is, the cult or ritualistic
aspects of Greek religion were never recorded systematically: instead, they existed in popular, living forms
that captured the mentality of the period and of the
society much more accurately than could the highly
intellectualized drama.[1] In spite of many commenta-
tors' attempts to concentrate on Hellenic mythology
alone, it is only one of the manifestations of myth,
and a derivative one at that. In addition to the
ceremonies of primitive peoples and to theater, there
are the motifs found in legends or folklore like those
in Camus' *Le Malentendu* or Giraudoux' *Ondine*.
There are fables or parables. There are the mythological archetypes—characters as well as situations—dis-
cernible in many genres and which are said to form an
integral part of contemporary life. Finally, a work
can be described as having a mythic structure—constructed as anthropologists or historians of religions
have postulated ancient myths to be constructed and
having roughly the same objective. The characteristic
upon which scholars appear to agree is that of a
return to the origins of existence, even if such a
return to the beginning may be homologized in any

1. Eliade, *Myth and Reality*, p. 158.

2. C. G. Jung
and C. Kerenyi,
*Essays on a
Science of
Mythology*
(New York:
Bollingen
Series, 22,
p. 10.
3. Mircea Eliade,
*Cosmos and
History* (New
York: Harper
Torchbooks,
1959), p. 85.

number of ways.[2] Although the cosmogony is its paradigm, it can entail the recovery of any source, whether of a natural occurrence, of art itself, or of the human personality. Hence, under the rubric "mythic structure" we can place such widely differing theories as those of Propp, Lévi-Strauss, Freud, Jung, or Lacan. There are, then, many definitions of myth and many conjectures as to its purpose. From the most frequently expressed opinions, one can deduce that it preserves archetypes or idealizations of human behavior, that it provides a model for the structure of reality or of society as well as for man's place in it, and that it explains how something came to be what it is. In it the constants or motifs of the collective unconscious are resumed, along with the recurring situations that constitute the human condition. Though the stories themselves appear to be instructive or descriptive, Eliade claims that the goal of primitive peoples in retelling them and in participating in rites which reenact them was to escape historical time and, consequently, the process of becoming.[3]

Judged by these criteria, Cocteau's work encompasses several mythic levels. First, recognition of a need for *divertissement* and for play (for a need to escape from time) dominates his essays as well as his art. Second, in the case of the child and, by extension, the poet, play becomes creation, which emanates from life's primitive roots by virtue of the poet's nature; myth consequently emerges as the only vehicle that can accommodate the intricate relationship between the artist and the real. Third, the structure of Cocteau's works frequently takes the form of a "return to the origins" which unveils the genesis of reality and of art. Such a structure elaborates a hero-mythology having the poet's situation in the world as its center. Fourth, the composition of myth as Cocteau seemed to have conceived it recapitulated that of reality: both were bipartite, formed by a synthesis of data in nature and consciousness (specifically, the poet's imagination). Finally, in addition to resuming Cocteau's view of the real, myth represents his most far-reaching attempt to come to terms with the world as he perceived it: his works imply that each artist-hero, by virtue of the models he presents to the public, has the potential for forming the perceptual modes that will succeed him in time.

On the most accessible level, myth as Cocteau used the word included any sort of device that provided an escape from time and from consciousness. "Mensonge," "inexactitude," and "fable" all fell into this broad interpretation of myth. In addition, the myth-making activity in general formed an element of human nature and served a human need: Cocteau often noted that people have "une soif d'irréalité."[4] They want to escape themselves and *la vie quotidienne*.

For the child and the poet, however, the term assumes much wider implications, because in these instances play reaches the level of a creative act. Artists' and children's games participate in the primeval eternal order of the universe. They emanate from a collective unconscious deposited in each human being but ultimately suppressed in everyone other than poets and the very young. In describing the nightly theater activities of Paul and Elizabeth

4. Cocteau, *Journal d'un inconnu*, p. 15.

5. Cocteau, *Les
Enfants terrib-
les*, p. 96.
6. Cocteau,
quoted in Rene
Dumesnil,
"Phèdre à
l'Opéra," in
R. Supp. 3.008,
Fonds Auguste
Rondel, Biblio-
thèque de
l'Arsenal.

in *Les Enfants terribles*, for example, the narrator
comments:

*Insistons encore, aucun des protagonistes de ce
théâtre et même celui tenant l'emploi de spectateur, n'avait conscience de jouer un rôle. C'était à
cette inconscience primitive que la pièce devait une
jeunesse éternelle. Sans qu'ils s'en doutâssent, la
pièce (ou chambre si l'on veut) se balançait au bord
du mythe.*[5]

Since they perpetuate recurring strands of our mental
heritage, certain types of art act as vehicles for racial
memory. Passed from generation to generation by
the artist, these currents reflect the kaleidoscope-
machine nature of the universe. Moreover, Cocteau
implies that without creators who can give the unconscious a form comprehensible to the public, racial
memory would be lost: "un mythe est un mythe
parce que les poètes le reprennent et l'empêchent de
mourir."[6] Therefore, art, myth (art in the most far-
reaching sense), consciousness, and "the real" constantly intertwine with and influence each other.

Clearly, in Cocteau's world the poet emerges as the
central figure in the synthesis that takes place between external reality and perception. The elaborate
mythology which lends continuity to his work and
from which his response to existence can be deduced
revolves around a recounting of the artist's fate in the
universe. The structure most frequently used to
illustrate his situation is that of a "return to the
origins," to the beginning of how he came to be what
he is. Two movements dominate the artist's condition:

his fall from grace and, much less certain, his salvation and revenge. Since motifs of the fall are homologous to any myth of the origins or of what existed *in illo tempore*, one must be careful to determine what constitutes "the beginning" for Cocteau. In traditional mythologies, for example, the explanation of the human condition is to be found in a sacred time before history: that man is now mortal or unhappy can be accounted for by the deeds of an archetypal ancestor like Adam, who determined the fate of all other human beings.[7] There was apparently a Golden Age before time as we know it, an epoch of timelessness and bliss. From this point of view, the sacred preceded the profane, and all models for behavior preexist man as we know him. Freud employed a similar sort of analysis in *Totem and Taboo* to arrive at the notion of a primal father-son conflict, and much of twentieth-century psychology is likewise characterized by a search for the roots of the self. Hence, investigations into what might be called the ultimate origins of a situation or of an individual personality supposedly reveal how something came to be what it is and, in the case of the motif of the fall, why there is no longer a paradise. Although Cocteau utilized the basic mythic structure of a return to the beginning, his modifications of the usual sacred-profane axis imply a radical questioning of values and perceptions as well as an affirmation of the artist's power. In fact, his concept of paradise is not even so remote as the psychoanalyst's prenatal or pre-weaning period. It is, rather, the entire period of childhood before man's social conformity and his lucidity. It is the time when the human being can be completely

7. Mircea Eliade, *Myths, Dreams and Mysteries* (New York: Harper Torchbooks, 1960).

8. Quoted in Gabriel d'Aubarède, "Rencontre avec Jean Cocteau," *Nouvelles littéraires*, 1928 (February 12, 1953), p. 1.
9. Cocteau, *Théâtre II*, p. 158.

himself without guilt or shame, when he is allowed to follow the contradictory instincts within him, when he is not divorced from the primeval forces in nature.

The significance of childhood in Cocteau's work can hardly be exaggerated. The poet constantly refered to "cette enfance à laquelle je n'échapperai jamais";[8] he urged his audience to suspend rational judgments and to react as if they were children at a Guignol show; he adapted fairy tales and created romantic legends. His first experiences with drama took place when he was a boy watching his mother dress for the theater and, later, when he was a spectator at the plays in which *monstres sacrés* such as de Max dominated the stage. With the passage of time, the great actors became almost mythological figures for him. Many of his heroes, in both novels and plays, are young: Thomas in *Thomas L'Imposteur*, Paul and Elizabeth in *Les Enfants terribles*, Hans in *Bacchus* and *Antigone*. In *La Machine à écrire*, Maxime says, "Mon enfance a été ma seule époque heureuse,"[9] and one suspects that this is Cocteau's own attitude. Wherever we turn in his writings, we find nostalgia for the Eden that preceded the responsibilities of adulthood, for the time when the human being existed in harmony with himself and with the world.

Cocteau apparently believed that each human being is born with tendencies which make him unique. All the opposing elements that form him constitute his pure self. As a child, he does nothing to suppress his urges, he follows his instincts and is in harmony with the world: not attempting to impose any preconceived notions on existence, he flows with the order of nature which he examines with awe, because he is seeing it for the first time. He is a primeval being in the sense that he exists as men did before the advent of society and its laws. Cocteau's interpretation of the child's world is almost identical to Nietzsche's conjecture of what the universe must have been like to primitive man:

10. Nietzsche, *Le Gai Savoir* (Paris: Gallimard, 1950), p. 188.

Le plus grand changement. *L'éclairage, les couleurs de tout ont bien changé! Nous ne comprenons plus bien comment les anciens hommes sentaient les choses les plus banales, les plus fréquentes, par exemple le jour et le réveil: comme ils croyaient aux rêves, la vie à l'état de veille avait pour eux une autre lumière . . . Tous les événements avaient une autre lumière, car un dieu rayonnait en eux; toutes les décisions aussi, toutes les prévisions lointaines: car on possédait des oracles, de secrets avertissements, et l'on croyait aux prédictions. La "Vérité" était sentie différemment, car le fou passait pour son interprète . . . Qu'était la joie au temps où l'on croyait au diable, au tentateur . . .*[10]

Since he is not limited by "normal" categories or perceptions of "the real," the child is sensitive to aspects of life hidden to the adult. Rather than being isolated from nature, then, he forms an integral part of it, and his relationship with the world is unmediated. For this reason, he enjoys a privileged sort of exchange with what is around him: his unbounded imagination manifests itself as a force equal to that of the exterior, it mingles with and controls the universe. If he plays, his game is transformed into reality; if he thinks himself a soldier or a king, he becomes one. In

that his will suffices to cast his existence into a form
resembling a work of art and, in some instances, to
perpetuate the work as truth in the eyes of others,
the child symbolizes the pinnacle of artistic creativity:
he channels and shapes the primeval, chaotic impulses
of nature.

Yet, as he grows older, his purity is contaminated
by society. He conforms to its explanations of the
universe, he begins to see reality only as his civilization sees it, he surrenders his ability to perceive the
world in all its magic. Thus he becomes out of joint
with the functioning of the cosmos, he loses his
power over it by suppressing his imagination, he
assigns goals and meaning where he had previously
accepted life without question.

Problems of morality and guilt are equally important. Cocteau often commented upon the conflicting
ethical rules of various times and countries, because
he felt they had no claim to universal validity: they
were merely an imposition on the course of things.
Therefore, his definition of morality—which specifically extols individualistic, defiant behavior that
remains true to the self—is opposed to any general
prescription for the good, and he condemned re-
course to a categorical imperative as a falsification of
the truth, a suppression of what is precious in the
individual. In relation to men's codes, the child is
amoral, and he is tolerated because he does not know
better; but upon reaching adulthood he becomes
socially responsible for his acts. Thus he is now held
guilty for disorders which were accepted as innocent
in his youth. If he varies greatly from civilized norms,
he is a criminal precisely because he is himself: his

very nature is condemned, he is predestined to be
guilty. If he does not conform, he is either ostracized
or put to death.

It is from Cocteau's conceptions of the child,
nature, morality, and society, then, that we can
determine his view of the human condition. First,
Cocteau defined man's social identity as a lie, a per-
version of his natural state. Consequently, morality
entailed being true to oneself. The natural course of
events, however, results in a loss of individuality and
in a conformity to general laws, and most human
beings make the transition between youth and
maturity without difficulty. They do not realize what
they have lost; they consider the behavior of a child
as disorder and their own standards as order.

In Cocteau's mythology, then, there is a breed of
heroes or superior men. They are the children, whatever their chronological age may be, who assert their
unique personalities. They refuse to compromise with
the demands of *"le pluriel"* or society; they persist in
being themselves; they reflect all the primitive, untamed forces of nature. From this point of view, it is
they who represent order, because they do not resist
the functioning of the universe-machine. Epitomized
by the artist, these heroes are what Cocteau calls
angéliques or *très purs*, without regard for the traditional connotations of the word "angel":

*Aussi, lorsque vous l'entendez dire d'un artiste, d'une
femme qu'ils sont angéliques, n'y cherchez pas l'ange
de vos images de première communion.*

*Désintéressement, égoisme, tendre pitié, cruauté,
souffrance des contacts, pureté dans la débauche,*

11. Cocteau, *Le Rappel à l'ordre*, p. 203.
12. Cocteau, *Journal d'un inconnu*, p. 30.
13. Cocteau, *Rappel à l'ordre*, p. 201.

mélânge d'un goût violent pour les plaisirs de la terre et de mepris pour eux, amoralité naive, ne vous y trompez pas: voila les signes de ce que nous nommons l'angélisme et que possède tout vrai poète, qu'il écrive, peigne, sculpte ou chante. Peu de personnes l'admettent, car peu de personnes ressentent la poésie.[11]

Such characteristics are natural in the child but are overcome in the adult. Their persistence challenges conventional definitions of crime: no natural sanction exists against incest or homosexuality. Only society has designated certain kinds of sexuality as wrong and right and has defined roles on the basis of sex. As Cocteau points out, nature itself is amoral and follows instincts without apology: "elle ne songe qu'à son ventre et à poursuivre une tâche invisible dont la visibilité démontre sa totale indifférence aux détresses de l'individu . . ."[12] Therefore, an angel is "un jeune animal éclatant, charmant, vigoureux,"[13] he is an androgynous creature; he is what aids the poet in maintaining his *ligne droite* or in being himself. If an author seeks a realism beyond the simple representation of what is ordinarily accepted as real, he will attempt to capture a situation from a much wider perspective than that of social truth. He will, in Nietzsche's phrase, go beyond good and evil; as Cocteau explained it,

C'est en vertu de ce principe que j'ai écrit: Genet est un moraliste et 'Je suis un mensonge qui dit toujours la vérité,' phrase dont les ânes firent leur herbe tendre. Ils s'y roulent. Cette phrase signifiait que

*l'homme est socialement un mensonge. Le poète
s'efforce de combattre le mensonge social surtout
lorsqu'il se ligue contre sa vérité singulière et l'accuse
de mensonge.*

    *Rien de plus âpre que cette défense du pluriel
contre le singulier. Les perroquets de toutes les cages
répètent: 'Il ment. Il dupe,' lorsqu'on s'acharne à ne
jamais mentir . . .*[14]

14. Cocteau,
Journal, p. 16.

Although a loss of purity is common to the human
condition, Cocteau was primarily interested in the
predicament of his angels who resist the fall into
society and who attempt to remain aloof from its
dictates. First, they are the only men to realize that
one is punished for being himself. They typify the
divided self, the human being who is torn between
what he is and his social responsibility. Second, their
efforts to communicate underscore man's essential
solitude, his inability to transcend social barriers once
they have been established. Third, they are always
faced with the choice of conformity or death; it is
through their conflicts with the order around them
that the spectator becomes aware that purity is impossible in the world as it is. Therefore, most of Cocteau's plays depict two states of being: that of grace
or of innocence and that which exists after the fall.

    There are few tragedies which could serve as more
appropriate vehicles for Cocteau's world view than
Sophocles' *Oedipus Rex*. Before Oedipus was born,
an oracle predicted that he would kill his father and
marry his mother. He himself heard the same prediction in his youth. His very essence, then, is to commit
parricide and incest. Willed by the gods, his "crimes"

15. Cocteau,
Théâtre I, p.
289.

are consistent with a universal order as well as with
his predetermined self. It is not only his "criminal"
characteristics which lead to his downfall, however.
One objective of the first three acts of *La Machine
infernale* is to give Oedipus an identity other than the
sketchy one provided by the myth, to underscore who
he was before he became a legendary figure. The
qualities that dominate are an absence of conventional proprieties and a determination to achieve
what he has set out to accomplish. He is a child
without a social identity obscuring his own, he does
not disguise his desires or ambitions. Clearly, in his
encounter with the Sphinx, he is interested only in
becoming King of Thebes: as Francis Fergusson
pointed out, he reacts like a thoughtless, selfish
adolescent. Oblivious of his debt to the monster, he
dashes off, thinking only of himself. He is primitive
and uncivilized, uncontaminated by niceties. The
playwright highlighted his character again in the last
act. Hearing of his "father's" death, Oedipus feigns
no sadness, because he believes that the prediction
about his killing his father can now never come true.
Likewise, when he learns that the King of Corinth is
not his real father, he refuses to stop his investigations until he learns who he is. "Que je sois fils des
muses ou d'un chemineau, j'interrogerai sans crainte,
je saurai des choses."[15] Significantly, the dilemma of
Oedipus' guilt lies at the center of *La Machine*. Cocteau drew the king's reaction to his deeds almost
verbatim from Sophocles' text:

Le Berger. *Tu es le fils de Jocaste, ta femme, et de
Laïus tué par toi au carrefour des trois routes.*

Inceste et parricide, les dieux te pardonnent.
Oedipe. *J'ai tué celui qu'il ne fallait pas. J'ai épousé
celle qu'il ne fallait pas. J'ai perpétué ce qu'il
ne fallait pas. Lumière est faite.*[16]

Yet, it is here, where *La Machine infernale* and
Oedipus Rex appear to merge, that Cocteau's personal myth most fully asserts itself, because it becomes evident that Oedipus did nothing but follow
the will of the gods; he did not go against their dictates. No ultimate moral order transcending society
judged him guilty; rather, the mores of his city condemned him, because he had gone beyond the limits
of permissible behavior. Even if one assumes that the
gods plotted against Oedipus in order to destroy him,
they did so by forming him in such a manner that he
would be guilty in Thebes' eyes: there was no divine
intervention in his punishment. This dichotomy between natural or divine order and a societal one
stands out clearly in a passage Cocteau added to the
Sophocles play:

Jocaste. *Oui, mon enfant, mon petit enfant . . . Les
choses qui paraissent abominables aux humains, si
tu savais, de l'endroit où j'habite, si tu savais
comme elles ont peu d'importance.*[17]

If Oedipus is abominable, he is so only to men. Obviously, such an interpretation conforms completely
to Cocteau's view of natural or pre-societal existence,
a sort of existence before condemnation, as it were, a
time when people had not interfered with the course of
things and decided what was right and wrong.

18. Cocteau,
Journal, p. 39.

La Machine infernale therefore highlights the
presence of two distinct orders: that of mankind or
society, and that of the universe. Together, they explain the human condition. When Oedipus was born,
he contained the seeds of what he would become. He
had the potential for what Cocteau named "les grands
désordres" which, he believed, provided an indication
of the superior human being. He in fact criticized
Freud for not having recognized how important "les
grands désordres" are: instead of eulogizing them, the
Viennese psychologist had placed them even more
firmly in the category of taboo:

*Il ne faudrait pas confondre la nuit dont je parle et
celle ou Freud invitait ses malades à descendre.
Freud cambriolait de pauvres appartements. Il en
démenageait quelques meubles médiocres et des
photographies érotiques. Il ne consacra jamais
l'anormal en tant que transcendance. Il ne salua pas
les grands désordres. Il procurait un confessionnal
aux fâcheux.*[18]

As Cocteau viewed the world, the destiny of any man
and especially of the outstanding person consists of
his being punished for whatever qualities differentiate
him from the average. In the course of existence, the
plural (the majority) always triumph over the singular; what is best for the many inevitably prevails.

As in the myth of Adam and Eve, Oedipus accepted
himself as guilty or impure when he gained knowledge: lucidity signaled the end of his childhood and
precipitated his fall. Until he discovered what he had
done, he had lived almost in a state of bliss. He

followed his own inclinations; his social identity was
in fact no different from his natural one. His kingdom
and his family prospered. During the whole of *Oedipus Rex* and *La Machine infernale*, the king's character does not change: like Adam and Eve, he does not
become any more or less evil than he was at the beginning. What does change is his perspective. He
knows something at the end of his investigations
that he did not know previously. As the Voice stated
before the fourth act, he became a man, and he did
this, interestingly enough, by learning that he was
guilty. What he understood was that he was no longer
a child, that he was expected to be responsive to his
country's ethics rather than to his own. After this
moment of redefinition (or of translation) when the
whole became visible to him for the first time, his
fall was complete: he could not return to what he had
been, he could never again be a child in his own
sphere of reference.

Although it unfolds in the same basic pattern, *Les
Chevaliers de la Table Ronde* differs from *La Machine
infernale* in two ways. First, no character represents
the "great disorder" of Oedipus and Jocasta. Second,
the triumph of the plural over the singular or of the
adult world over that of the child is much more
clearly developed. The "return to the origins" is just
as obvious, however, because, as noted above in
Chapter 1, Arthur had reverted to a childlike existence during the first act of the play: because of
Merlin's spell, he could gambol with Ginifer and
neglect his responsibilities as ruler. As is the case with
any magic, however, the enchanter's power had to
come to an end. Like Oedipus, Arthur was not content

19. Cocteau,
Théâtre I, p.
397.
20. Ibid., pp.
409–410.
21. Ibid., p. 412.

with half-truths; he wanted to proceed as far as he could into knowledge of a situation that concerned him. When he began to suspect that his wife had not been faithful to him, he questioned her without pity, just as Oedipus had queried the messenger. In fact, he almost repeated the Theban king's words: "je veux savoir et je saurai . . ."[19] During one harrowing night when he discovered the lovers together and killed Lancelot, his illusions were destroyed. Like the child who for the first time becomes aware of deception, he learned that even "Gauvain," whom he had so adored, helped Guenièvre conceal the adulterous meetings.

Although Arthur discovered no unwittingly committed crime, he nevertheless, like Oedipus, experienced a coming of age. He realized, finally, that he could not accept those around him without question, that they were not what they appeared to be. Society won, since each character ultimately has to play by its rules rather than by his own. An understanding of conventions and a conformity to them signal the end of childhood. Natural impulses are stifled, and one's mask becomes his identity. Arthur's adventure was an interlude, a short return to the childhood paradise. Although the king thought that he could revert to innocence, such a reversal is, of course, impossible, since the child's purity cannot last in the world.

The final break with youth lies in assuming responsibility, and Arthur must also take this step: "Je dois rendre compte de mes actes."[20] Galaad warns him that seeing the truth about the inevitable order of the universe is painful: "La vérité commence. Elle est dure. Elle vous fera mal au réveil."[21] If it can be said that Cocteau expressed any truth in his play, it is "Il faut payer, payer toujours. Payer de sa personne et de ses actes."[22] The original sin of man, it seems, is not to be found in a primeval flaw; it lies, rather, in the fact that a society needs lies and restrictions on the disorders of nature in order to survive. It requires an alteration of natural inclinations. The necessity of disguises and the relinquishing of individual freedom and identity immediately follow. Even if one somehow hides his flaws, he must always feel guilty for their existence. Responsibilities destroy the paradise of childhood, and man grows up to be a social creature instead of a fully developed personality. For each refinement of civilization, he must pay with a part of himself.

Although Cocteau has disparaged *Les Monstres sacrés* as a play in which he did not "engage his substance,"[23] it nevertheless contains some of his most precise statements on the processes that force individuals to assume behavior that is not their own, and on the loss of innocence and purity. Esther is easily identified as the uncompromised, uncorrupted character, since she wears no mask at the beginning of the play: her orientation was that of a child and she had youth's naive, impetuous nature. Moreover, her morality did not conform to an ethic accepted by a majority of society; it was uniquely her own. Discovery of her husband's infidelity, however, initiates the actress into adulthood. Believing him to be as honest as she is, she had trusted him implicitly. For the first time she realizes that people are not what they seem: they all play roles; they conceal their true thoughts and feelings beneath an elaborate network

22. Ibid., p. 418.
23. Cocteau/Fraigneau, *Entretiens avec André Fraigneau*, p. 135.

24. Cocteau,
Théâtre II, p. 32.
25. Ibid., p. 39.
26. Ibid., p. 5.

of lies. Like any child she learns the distinction between being and appearance, between the glittering surface of things and their sordid reality: "Je croyais que la vie ressemblait à certaines cartes postales. Je viens de comprendre que je me trompais. Je ne comprenais rien. J'ai compris."[24] Even after she understands that Liane has lied to her about being Florent's mistress, she cannot regain her childlike attitude. She can no longer accept her happiness without suspicion.

By opposing Esther's natural inclinations or *morale* to the deception which characterizes ordinary human relationships, Cocteau underscores the futility of the individual's struggle against *le pluriel*. Instead of divorcing or leaving her husband, the actress brings Liane to their home as her student. She encourages the *ménage à trois*, loves her pupil, and waits for Florent's infatuation to pass. Understanding that her reaction is bizarre, she is nevertheless unable to behave like *tout le monde*, because at this point the forces that make her what she is still determine her conduct: "Il y a des forces qui nous poussent vers la catastrophe . . ."[25] When, at the end of the play, she has to resort to acting in order to win Florent back, she has in fact lost the purity of her childhood. She becomes like everyone else and conforms to a pattern that suppresses her own personality. In his notes for the interpretation of parts, Cocteau emphasizes that she has lost her sincerity:

Le reste du rôle est d'une femme d'amour, maladroite et noble. A la fin, elle a 'beaucoup appris.' Elle se souvient de ses rôles. Sa sincérité se teinte d'un peu de théâtre.[26]

Although the last seconds of the action are taken up
by wild laughter that represents *"la détente d'une
farce de théâtre après cinq mois d'énervement tragique,"*[27] it is impossible to think that the relationship
of the two *monstres sacrés* will never be what it was
before Liane's arrival. Esther is now aware of a part
of life that she did not know before; she is no longer
a trusting child. Her attitude not only toward Florent
but also toward existence itself has changed. She will
from now on wonder and doubt, assume a role, and
hide her emotions. The final impression left by the
play is that this superficial gaiety was all the actress
had ever had, that, in fact, her confidence in love was
only the naiveté of an adolescent. If nothing about
her situation has changed, her perspective is different
from that at the beginning, and her resigned solitude
is the only answer possible for her.

Perhaps no play of Cocteau has been as contro-
versial as *Les Parents terribles*. The problem is one
of definition, and the resulting confusion strength-
ens Cocteau's claims of the deforming tendencies of conventional morality. Man's narrow systems
make him blind to everything except what he wants
to see he said, and he predicted many outraged
reactions to his work. In fact, he intended to shock
the public. He described his play in the following
terms:

Les Parents terribles *sont à mes yeux la pureté même.
Il y a une atmosphère close où le mal n'entre pas, où
la question du bien et du mal ne se pose même pas.
C'est la ressemblance de cette pièce avec le roman des
Enfants terribles.*[28]

27. Ibid., p. 79.
28. Cocteau/Fraig-
neau, *Entretiens*, p.
133.

29. Cocteau,
Théâtre I, pp.
434-435.

As he explains, the work is not concerned with good
or evil; rather, it depicts a family in which the moral
code of each member is personal and dependent upon
his own desires or inclinations. In a sense, then, it is
a return to nature.

The only character in *Les Parents terribles* who is
not impulsive and pure is Léonie, the adult. She
represents the existence of an order imposed arbi-
trarily on life. As a detached observer of the rest of
her family, she plays a role that hides her emotions.
Even her stylish clothing contrasts with the others'
lack of concern for appearances.

Georges, Michel, and Yvonne are children. They live
without pretense and expect the same of those
around them. Like Cocteau's *angéliques*, they are
selfish and disinterested at the same time. From the
point of view of society, they are amoral. The distinction between the adults and the children of the play
is made in the first act:

Leo. *Je ne suis pas méchante, je t'observe depuis hier,
    Yvonne, et je me félicite d'avoir apporté un peu
    d'ordre dans la roulotte. En ce monde il y a les en-
    fants et les grandes personnes. Je me compte, helas,
    parmi les grandes personnes. Toi . . . Georges . . . Mik,
    vous êtes de la race des enfants qui ne cessent jamais
    de l'être, qui commettraient des crimes . . .*[29]

Leo is the only adult in a child's *roulotte*, which is
Yvonne's pet term for the apartment and which
evokes the freedom and independence of gypsies.
Such people exist outside of society's laws because
they refuse to be part of a larger, more regimented

system. Therefore, Georges, Yvonne, and their son
lead an unstructured life. Georges invents gadgets that
never work, Yvonne rarely leaves her bed, and Michel
drifts from interest to interest.

Although Michel's fiancée Madeleine represents
order, she, unlike Léo, is true to herself and therefore pure. She and Léonie resemble each other superficially by their passion for neatness, which in the
aunt is imposed upon her character without resulting
from it. On a deep level, then, Madeleine, like Esther,
like any of Cocteau's "angels," belongs to the children's realm, since she refuses to compromise her
"line" at the same time that she admits her amorality:

Madeleine. *Je hais le mensonge. Le moindre men-*
songe me rend malade. J'admets qu'on se taise ou
qu'on s'arrange pour faire le moins de peine possible.
Mais, le mensonge . . . le mensonge de luxe! Je ne me
place pas au point de vue de la morale, je suis tres
amorale. J'ai l'intuition que le mensonge fausse des
mécanismes qui nous dépassent, qu'il dérange des
ondes, qu'il détraque tout.[30]

What threatens Yvonne's way of life is not so much
an antagonistic society as a natural relationship
challenging her position. The very animal nature of
the mother is such that she cannot accommodate herself to anything but her own desires; she is compelled
to follow her emotions even if they destroy her.
When she sees the new family composed of Madeleine,
Michel, Georges, and Léo, she feels that there is no
longer a place for her, that she has lost all that

31. Cocteau, *Les Enfants terribles*, p. 110.
32. Ibid., p. 147.

mattered to her in the world, and she takes an overdose of insulin. Capable of analyzing her objectively, Léo understands that her sister could never live a compromised existence in which she would be prevented from being completely herself and in which she could not totally dominate the life of her son.

Like *Les Enfants terribles, Les Parents terribles* is one of Cocteau's most personal works. In both the novel and the play the characters are children, regardless of age. They live according to their own ethic in a game which, to them, is reality. They dwell in a dimly lit, primeval world outside the realm of societal laws: "Il est de ces maisons, de ces existences qui stupéfieraient les personnes raisonnables."[31] Unlike the novel, however, where "le génie de la chambre veillait"[32] and Elizabeth's husband is killed before he can contaminate the purity of the household, Yvonne's world is destroyed by the presence of an outsider: the mother has no means of preventing her child from becoming an adult. Instead of choosing conformity, as Esther does, she chooses death, for she is much more impetuous than the actress, much closer to nature's savagery and to that of the very young child. Unable to have her way, she becomes spiteful, but she has no chance to reverse her decision. This *pureté farouche* which tolerates no compromise is unique to Cocteau's theater, since it is almost impossible to present such a hermetic universe on the stage. Yet it does not approach the brutality of *Les Enfants terribles*, where mythological child-gods drive each other to an inevitable death, and where the world of play excludes everything outside itself.

In *L'Aigle à deux têtes* and *Renaud et Armide*,

social identity makes purity impossible and thus leads
to the ultimate solitude of the individual. Discussing
Renaud et Armide with Andre Fraigneau, Cocteau explained that "c'était le thème de la solitude des
êtres qui se devinent sans se voir et qui n'arrivent pas
à se rejoindre lorsqu'ils se voient."[33] In becoming
human, Armide lost her purity: she insisted on
viewing Renaud as a king—that is, a social identity.
She fell, as it were, from her existence as precivilized
spirit where conventions lacked importance. Likewise, the game conceived by the Queen in *L'Aigle*
came to an end when it was countered by the world
as it is: neither protagonist could remain pure from
what society had defined him to be.

As we mentioned earlier, the motifs on which
Antigone and *Bacchus* are based resemble each other
closely. Since the theme of the persecuted artist recurs frequently throughout Cocteau's work, it is not
surprising that myths of saints and of martyrs fascin-
ate him: "tous les saints désobéissent aux lois exis-
tantes et c'est pourquoi on les torture."[34] *Bacchus*,
however, unfolds specifically around the problems of
youth, the passage from individuality to social
identity, and the choice between conformity and
death.

In *Journal d'un inconnu*, Cocteau explained his objective in writing *Bacchus*:

*J'abordai le thème du désarroi de la jeunesse au
milieu des dogmes, des sectes, des obstacles qu'on
lui oppose. En proie aux offres de service et aux
sentiments, elle cherche à rester libre. Sa liberté
désordonnée se glisse entre les obstacles jusqu'à*

33. Cocteau/Fraig-
neau, *Entretiens*,
p. 151.
34. Cocteau, *Entre-
tiens avec Roger
Stéphane*, p. 18.

35. Cocteau,
Journal, p. 87.
36. Eliade, *Myth
and Reality*, pp.
21ff.

*ce qu'elle s'y écrase. Elle ne saurait vaincre que par la
ruse ou par une prise de pouvoir. L'adresse lui fait
défaut que le méandre exige. Elle fonce. Sa maladroite ligne droite, son audace, son coeur, ses sens, la
desservant dans une société où règne le méandre, où
les méandres s'entrecroisent et s'affrontent sourde-
ment.*[35]

Moreover, he revealed that he adapted the week of
disorder, which is the play's setting, from a custom
that continues at Veney during harvest time and
which has its source in a Sumerian ritual. Eliade
analyzes such rituals as a return to the primeval chaos
from which the universe and humanity will be "re-
born" at the end. They are examples of symbolic
regression to a time before history and duration; they
give hope of cosmic renewal.[36]

The peasant Hans, who was chosen to be Bacchus,
incarnates primitive chaos. He has no system; he follows only his inclinations and desires, which at times
are contradictory. Like other Coctelian heroes, he is
a youth who has refused to submit to the categorical
imperative. Opposing him is the established order of
the church. It is evident that his reign of chaos or
purity offers only an interlude like childhood itself.
The town has armed itself against Hans and is prepared
to murder him the instant the festivities end. Since it
is impossible that he continue to exist as he is, he has
two choices. He can sign an abjuration for his actions
and enter the Catholic orders, or he can face the
crowd and, thus, certain death. Signing the paper
would represent his capitulation to society. At the
end of the play he throws himself to the crowd.

From Cocteau's use of a symbolic return to the origins and of a triumph of the previously existing order, it is apparent that at least within the context of the play, the emergence of a different world where each person can determine his own order was not possible. The forces of *le pluriel* prevailed over the individual or *le singulier*. By a ritualistic new beginning which really perpetuates the old system, the author underscored the fact that such a fall into organized society is the order of the human condition, that no other path is possible.

It appears, then, that the motif of the fall is the thread linking the diverse faces of Cocteau's theater. Each play is structured as a return to the origins of the human condition, each one explains why reality is as it is and how it came to be. At least one character is "pure" in the Coctelian sense of the word. Whatever his age, he remains true to himself and follows his own morality instead of society's. At the same time, he is aware of powerful forces that control the development of events, and he shys away from what he calls "disturbing the mechanisms of it all." For a while (the time of his "beginning," so to speak), he exists in the blissful state of childhood, where there are no lies and where he accepts everything around him as if it were what it seemed. Then, one day, he discovers that he has been living an illusion: like Adam and Eve, he gains knowledge. He may, like Oedipus, learn that he is guilty of crimes he never intended or, like Esther, that those around him are not what he thought. Stanislas realizes that he and the Queen are alienated by their social identities, and Arthur reluctantly accepts his responsibilities as king.

37. Cocteau,
Foyer des artistes,
p. 154.
38. Cocteau,
Journal, p. 88.

The images that recur are those of fire and blindness:
each character is unable to see the truth. "Yvonne,
c'est un feu qui se détruit."[37] The Cardinal warns Hans,
vous courez au feu comme un papillon de nuit."

Reasoning from Cocteau's definition of "angélisme," we can say that most of his plays recount the
fall of an angel. In each work it appears that the will
of the many invariably triumphs over le *singulier,*
that the "great disorders" are suppressed. Yet in Cocteau's mythology, as in many others, there is a
redemption. Cocteau has said of Orphée that "il joue
à qui perd gagne, alors que ceux qui servent le visible
ne peuvent jouer qu'à qui gagne perd."[38] He means
that although Orpheus loses his struggle with the
Bacchants or society, he and his poetry ultimately prevail. It does not appear to be true, however, as is frequently assumed, that he and Eurydice, or any of the
lovers in Cocteau's plays, are united after death and
ascend to Heaven, where they are rewarded or justified.
Rather, it is through myth—which in Cocteau's vocabulary is equivalent to the highest form of art—that the
artist can have his revenge by gaining control over
reality's processes, and that fragmentation may be overcome. Through the centuries it is Oedipus and Orpheus
who emerge as heroes and are admired by a society
like the one that persecuted them, a society that applauds
their great disorder even as it persecutes their modern
counterparts. In a reversal of myth and history effected
by the poet, the child-anarchist becomes an ideal, an
object of awe, instead of an outcast. Unlike anyone
else but a child, the artist has the capacity to pro-
pose models that will be imitated and perpetuated
to such an extent that they will ultimately assume a

position tantamount to that held by "essence" in a
perceptual mode (now past) where meaning and
stability were possible. The poet, consequently, takes
the place gods occupied previously: he controls man's
view of reality and makes existence bearable.

That Cocteau's answer lay in myth resulted from
the analogy he obviously drew between its structure
and reality's. As shown in Chapter 2, he perceived the
real as being wholly constituted neither by external
data nor by consciousness: its totality resides in the
synthesis of the two, and owing to the nature of perception and of time, such a synthesis can have no
claim to any kind of absolute existence. Consequently,
he intuited reality as split or fragmented: no essence
preexists phenomena and gives them an immutable
character. Art also represents a synthesis, since it is
composed by data in the collective unconscious and
the artist's unique personality. Myth, as Cocteau
defined it, offered him a means of overcoming fragmentation, since, in addition to fulfilling a human
need for diversion and to reflecting deep mental configurations, it epitomizes the dialectical relationship
that characterizes reality: it brings together history
(fact) and imagination or desire. With the poet as
intermediary, however, it does so in such a way that
the two elements (objectivity and subjectivity) form
a stable union which, unlike others, can endure in
time. Probably because they correspond to elements
in the collective unconscious, certain events or historical figures, for example, have the quality of appealing
to the popular imagination. As people sensitive to this
form of *poésie à l'état brut*, artists (or myth-makers)
through the ages can infuse history with their own

39. Ibid., p. 119.   subjectivity until what is believed as true is not what
really happened but, rather, the version that poets
choose to perpetuate. Power resides in the ability to
make one's own perspective prevail, to link objectivity
and subjectivity in such a way that they are no longer
divided. Therefore, in the course of history, fable
supplants fact, and the artist emerges as essential to
mankind's interpretation of the real. In this way,
myth both epitomizes and resolves the contradictory
forces at play in Cocteau's world because paradoxical
elements—sometimes interspersed across the years as
the legend evolves toward its final form—can exist in
equilibrium. Cocteau often called poetry a religion
without hope which, like all others, protects its
secrets through allegories or fables. Since, in his
opinion, truth is in some sense protected by the interplay of illusion and reality, the myth or legend—
which puts truth into a code—aptly recaptures the
structure of his vision: it is the way of explaining the
world that is by its nature multipartite. It is a story
and it is fact; it satisfies man's need for illusion and
for truth.

The relationship between myth and history evoked
by the structure of Cocteau's works highlights a radical departure from a traditional world view according
to which meaning preexists being. To the religious or
primitive man, myths are true because a supposedly
immutable, primordial substratum of existence has
somehow been revealed to human beings, usually
through divine intervention or through the messages
of holy men. It is this substratum that provides a
model for the structure of the universe and for man's
behavior.[39] For Cocteau, however, no value-giving

source exists outside consciousness; there are no preexisting forms behind the chaos, no sacred time before
history. The layer of the sacred has been abolished.
At the starting point of each of his fables, there is
nothing outside man's present historical sphere;
human beings do not have illustrious origins; they
were always mortal, always limited; there has never
been anything more, no paradise, no Golden Age;
there is no ultimate meaning. The very stuff of the
traditional fable is destroyed. Moreover, though he
utilized the basic myths in western civilization in his
work, his treatment of them implies that they are
false in any kind of factual sense. They have grown
and evolved through human desire, through people's
tendencies to accept what they would like to believe,
rather than from an objective or defensible basis.
Whereas in religious thought, archetypal forms precede man, chaos precedes the artist's forms. Whereas
traditionally the nature of history and of profane
time can be explained by and patterned on revela-
tions of what took place in the beginning, to Cocteau
there is no beginning, there is only the functioning of
the machine, there is only history. Thus history itself
is the starting point of myth. Instead of preexisting,
form is brought from chaos by the powers of the
artist.

The structure of *La Machine infernale* provides the
most striking example of such a position. Cocteau
literally returned to the beginning, to a beginning
without form and without divine archetypes. Since
origins lie in history, he depicted the man Oedipus
was before he became idealized through the process
of legend; he painted a Thebes like any city in any

age, he gave a prominent role to the common person
and his eternal problems. The source of ideals and
beauty, he implied, is to be found in commonplace
(or worse) situations transformed during the centuries.
In Sophocles' *Oedipus Rex*, incest represents a monstrous, extraordinary crime, but Cocteau went beyond the mere naming of horror. His third-act
bedroom scene brings to life all that is grotesque,
sordid, and ugly in the mother-son relationship.
Therefore, the spectator cannot escape the physical
reality before him: he is forced to witness an aspect
of the legend heretofore only verbalized, and at this
moment he is inescapably face to face with history.
The tawdry facets of *La Machine infernale* are delib-
erate. Instead of pandering to his audience with
Boulevard techniques, as is often claimed, the playwright in fact drew upon the only type of theater
suitable to his aims. His taking advantage of the
Parisian audience's acquaintance with situation
comedies based on an older woman and her gigolo
reduced alienation from what was happening on the
stage. Since Oedipus and Jocasta were not yet tragic
characters, the spectator had to see a contemporary
form of drama, one with which he was familiar.

On the other hand, Act IV represents the starting
point of myth. Rather than equating this act with
Sophocles' *Oedipus Rex*, one should view it as a
source or paradigm of all treatments of Oedipus. Had
the crimes of Jocasta and the king not been so monstrous, or had they remained undiscovered and un-
punished, the fulfillment of the oracle would have
remained trivial. As Tiresias stated many times,
however, destiny must be played out to its unbearable

end. The unmasking of parricide and incest immediately exiled mother and son from any societal order, but at the same time, the two main characters transcended the category of ordinary criminals. Through their suicide and self-inflicted blindness, they brought to its culmination what Tiresias calls "un chef-d'oeuvre d'horreur,"[40] and through disorder of an almost inconceivable immensity they free themselves from average status in the world: "Votre police est bien faite, Creon; mais où cet homme se trouve, elle n'aurait plus le moindre pouvoir."[41] When Oedipus, Antigone, and Jocasta leave Thebes, they are beginning a journey through time, a journey which begins with the proto-myth that is Act IV and that liberates them from the condemnation of ordinary men like Creon:

Tiresias. *Ils ne t'appartiennent plus; ils ne relèvent
    plus de ta puissance.*
Creon. *Et à qui appartiendraient-ils?*
Tiresias. *Au peuple, aux poètes, aux coeurs purs.*[42]

From age to age, artists will be intrigued by the nature of the situation; they will give it form, and the form will triumph over a sordid history that will be forgotten. Out of chaos and mediocrity (such as Creon's) great disorder will be transformed into works of art that vindicate and praise the antisocial. For this reason Jocasta rather than Antigone leads Oedipus in Cocteau's version: instead of a king (that is, a socially responsible man), he must be remembered as a child, a being who in fact has no ties to a narrow civilized system.

To a differing degree, both *Orphée* and *Bacchus*

40. Eliade, *Myth and Reality*, pp. 19ff.
41. Cocteau, *La Machine infernale* (Paris: Larousse, n.d.), p. 132.
42. Ibid., p. 133.

43. Cocteau,
Théâtre I, p.
130.

raise the question of the relationship between history
and art. In *Orphée*, for example, Cocteau appears to
be playing with the idea of historical origins, of what
Orpheus was before he actually became the poet we
imagine him to be. Part of the goal of the play is to
indicate his errors with the horse, to demonstrate that
poetry is *expiration* instead of *inspiration*, hence to
explain why Orphée was not yet a "real" poet. From
this point of view, Heurtebise becomes an angel by
Cocteau's definition rather than a purely Christian
attachment to a Greek legend: he is the one who turns
Orpheus inward toward the self, who helps him "follow his line." If this interpretation is correct, the sentence, "J'espère un jour charmer les vraies bêtes,"[43]
is not completely farcical. It is, in addition, a hint
to the audience that it is seeing only the potential
Orpheus of legend, the man he was before he attained
the status of poet.

   The conclusion of *Bacchus* stands out as one of the
most interesting examples of mythic structure, because at the end of the play Cocteau deliberately
highlighted the link between History and legend. In
order that Hans be remembered as a heretic, a person
who revolted against the established order, Lothar
shot him. Yet in an attempt to use the young man's
death for his own cause, the Cardinal celebrated Hans
as a Christian martyr, a person who had died after
accepting the faith. The play's ending remains ambiguous because it in effect depicts a contest between
groups of signs that will be remembered through the
centuries: no one can know whether Hans' or the
Cardinal's manipulation of data will prevail. It is as if
Cocteau opposed not only myth and history but also

possible configurations of facts in order to emphasize
the malleability and fluidity of the real. By doing this,
he also underscored both the grandeur and the pre-
cariousness of the artist's state. In a world where all
values arise in the perceiving consciousness (hence,
the essential ambiguity of the real), but where, because of the nature of the universe, a single consciousness cannot acquire authority or control, the position
Cocteau chose was that of the work of art as a
counterforce to existence. The artist can create his
own forms, he can play games that rival and sometimes replace the flimsy givens of history. In gaining
credence, myths insidiously overthrow bourgeois
social values, it is true. More deeply, however, they
weave themselves into the very fabric of reality, with
the result that they have equal (sometimes superior)
worth in the eyes of those who come into contact
with them; they challenge and frequently dominate
the banal, deterministic character of life. At the same
time, the artist's creations are subject to the same
flux or lack of independent essence as anything else
in the world: a man like the Cardinal who is determined to use them can change their form and destroy
what a poet has so carefully constructed. Chance can
do the same thing:

*Il est très probable que le travail du poète est une
projection de graines, c'est un travail beaucoup plus
naturel qu'on ne le pense, un travail de plante. Les
graines tombent où elles peuvent, il y en a qui
prennent, il y en a qui ne prennent pas.*[44]

History's becoming myth offers redemption not

44. Cocteau/Fraig-
neau, *Entretiens
avec André Fraig-
neau*, pp. 65–66.

45. Eliade,
*Cosmos and
History*, p. 34.

only for the artist. As Cocteau stated many times, man has a deep need for form because he is not comfortable in the constant flux of existence. In his daily life as well as in his contacts with art itself, he turns to ideals and beauty proffered by the poet.

First, even if only subconsciously, the average person senses that his existence is insufficient, and, no longer able to create his own forms, he adopts those of the artist. The implication of Cocteau's view of myth is that in their lives human beings attempt to imitate archetypes perpetuated through the centuries by art, that they do not view their actions as meaningful unless they conform to these models.

In Cocteau's work this necessity and desire for form are represented by mythomaniacs who vainly attempt to transform their lives into art. Characters in *La Machine à écrire* and *Les Monstres sacrés*, for example, play games with the desperate hope that, somehow, they will become reality, that an esthetically pleasing fiction will change into fact. Taking advantage of a series of anonymous letters, both Margot and Maxime pretend to be "La Machine à écrire" in an effort to make themselves interesting. Similarly, Liane, the young actress, confessed that she pretended to be Florent's mistress so that she might escape her mediocrity. She wanted to imitate Esther's style and mode of existence which to her incarnated an ideal. Such behavior closely resembles Eliade's definition of the primitive ontological conception: nothing has meaning or even reality unless it imitates a model or an archetype.[45] As is evident, each character thinks his existence lacks value unless it conforms to the archetypes provided by art, and he believes in his own reality only insofar as he attains his ideal. Rather than some divine, eternal model preceding history, then, it is the artist's work, the esthetically pleasing life, that supplies patterns for what man calls reality.

If we accept the conclusion that many of Cocteau's plays trace the evolution from history to myth or legend, it appears that they should simultaneously reveal the general characteristics that distinguish art from life as it is now when creation and existence are no longer one: the first three acts of *La Machine infernale* are as much a return to the origin of the Oedipus myth (that is, of art) as they are an explanation of the human condition. At the very center of Cocteau's work is obviously the question of what constitutes the difference between art and existence, of why nature itself or a mere imitation thereof is not art, of what is necessary to transform the commonplace into an act of creation. That one of his earliest theoretical writings, the preface to *Les Mariés de la Tour Eiffel* (1921), has as its subject the perpetual interrelation of the banal and the sublime, the constant passing from one level to another, underscores his lifelong striving to understand how something comes to be perceived as an art object. The criteria to be inferred from Cocteau's own work are those of esthetic distance (comparable to Bullough's psychical distance), intensity or concentrated time, and a form that captures the multidimensional nature of reality.

As is evident from the assumption that myth evolves from history, a temporal as well as a spatial distance between fact and its representation is a necessary condition of art. To a certain extent, the

46. Cocteau,
Théâtre II, p.
327.

farther one is from an event or an individual, the
greater the possibility of viewing it as a coherent
entity: patterns and symmetry become more evident,
and features hidden by the proximity of the observer
take on new meaning. What is highly individualized
or intricate becomes an ideal, many more degrees
removed from the everyday world than an attempted
imitation would be.

Almost as if in compensation for the rather gener-
alized portrayal of characters or events, time is of an
intensity and concentration that in themselves imply
the extraordinary. The Queen in *L'Aigle à deux têtes*
explains for example, "Il faut assassiner vite et dehors.
Il faut assassiner vite et être lapidé par la foule.
Sinon le drame retombe et tout ce qui retombe est
affreux."[46] Somewhat similar to the *in medias res*
construction of a Racine tragedy, the span of time
presented to the spectator is composed of highly
significant moments while the accelerated pace of the
action reinforces the impression of excitement, of a
frenzy that one might feel before a storm.

The ultimate effect of both distance and intensity is
that of the attainment of form: whereas existence in
general—in that it has no real beginning or end since
it is always in process—is amorphous, art fixes its
diverse aspects from the unique viewpoint of the
artist. As in a child's game whose components are
nature and fantasy, the commonplace is juxtaposed
with the mysterious in such a fashion that there is an
almost perfect equilibrium between them. One of the
best illustrations of such an esthetic, which Cocteau
describes as that of the "plus vrai que le vrai" is
Picasso's bull's head composed of the seat and handle-

bars of a bicycle. While the work is formed from two easily identifiable objects, it is nevertheless obviously more: imagination can release the potential of what at first glance might appear to be completely banal and limited. The work of art, then, reveals all that transcends adult experience, all the passion, beauty, ugliness, and violence inaccessible to normal perception and hidden by the stultifying framework of habit.

If our analysis is correct, the key to understanding Cocteau's conceptions of art lies in his use and creation of myths, because only in myth could all the facets of his perceptual mode be reconciled: the kaleidoscope-like mechanisms, the fluidity, and the ultimate gratuitousness of his world were postulated and responded to through mythic structures. On an immediate level, the experience of myth-as-theater (whether "theater" means actual presentation as during performance of a play or implies the creation of games, as in *Thomas l'Imposteur* or *Les Enfants terribles*) suspends self-consciousness or lucidity while participants enjoy a nonalienated relationship with a world created by the imagination. On a much more precarious plane, the outcast (poet, martyr, saint) may at last attain to an order with which he is in harmony and which avenges him. The Janus-faced third act of *La Machine infernale* represents the epitome of the double and of its resolution in Cocteau's work. Rooted in the *boulevard* tradition, in derision, in teasing, in all that is sordid, tawdry and cheap, nevertheless, as a completely ambiguous sign, it functions as the birth of myth and of liberation. It contains the seed of art.

5. Consciousness and Power

1. Jean-Paul Sartre, "Auto-portrait à 70 ans," *Le Nouvel Observateur*, 55 (June 30–July 7, 1975), p. 76.

Par exemple, j'aimais bien Cocteau, que j'avais connu en 1944, et que j'ai souvent vu jusqu'à la fin: j'ai dîné avec lui quelques jours avant sa mort. Je le trouvais très sympathique, et beaucoup moins clown qu'il ne l'est dans la vie qu'on lui attribue maintenant.

C'est lui surtout qui parlait. Il parlait de sa manière de voir le monde, de ses idées—que je ne suivais jamais qu'un tout petit peu, parce qu'il était superficiel, selon moi. Il était très brillant causeur, il avait de la sensibilité, mais peu d'idées. Ce qui ne veut pas dire que je ne le tienne pour un poète de grande valeur.[1]

Few artists of our time can have greater claim to the title "poet" than can Jean Cocteau. What Sartre's evaluation of him (with its implicit distinction between "poetry" and "philosophical discourse") appears to indicate is not so much that he lacked ideas but, rather, that he was a man who communicated by means of images instead of arguments, that his very mode of expression remained evocative and indirect instead of rational and assertive. It is difficult to know whether to take Cocteau literally when he stated, as he often did, that thought makes action

impossible (a phrase he borrowed from Nietzsche) or
when he rejected Cartesian logic as a road to knowledge, but in every genre as well as in every individual
work he proceeded intuitively—poetically. His relationship with the universe seems to have developed
out of emotion and sensitivity rather than logic, and
his portrayal of reality consequently appealed to, and
was based on, feeling. He never claimed to be an intellectual; his art should not be judged as intellectual
art: the antithesis of Sartre, Montherlant, and almost
any other twentieth-century French artist, he appears
to have enjoyed little distance or protection from the
world. Unable to circumscribe knowledge within
reason's safe, neat compartments, and incapable of
self-assured control over his environment, he attempted to play games with the unknown, to cajole it into
a kind of truce. He could not have expressed ideas as
Sartre did because he did not enjoy the same sort of
relationship with reality. Whereas Roquentin, for
example, could detach himself from a gratuitous,
chaotic existence and analyze it (hence, be master of
it in some sense), Cocteau remained emprisoned almost entirely within it. Therefore, his mode of expression (his "hieroglyphs") frequently reflected a
pre-analytic stance vis-à-vis experience. The "portrait" his work leaves us, then, is one of a sensitivity
rather than an intellect.

His art reveals highly persistent structures of ambiguity and of a difficultly maintained equilibrium.
The unstable characteristics underlying what he
created result from his poetry's having its genesis in
irrational forces which the poet was able to exterior-
ize in the form of art but with which he could never

2. Cocteau, *Le Secret professionnel* (Paris: Stock, 1948), p. 225.

ultimately come to terms. Each work consequently represents a temporary rather than a definitive accommodation with the real, and the total opus emerges not as the picture of a development or of an evolution but as a series of causally unconnected postures. Therefore, the consciousness behind the whole appears to have been primarily an object (an entity acted upon), rather than a subject within the context of his world.

Wherever we look in Cocteau's esthetic, we find evidence of a mental set shaped by an intuition of contingency. In praising night or the unconscious, he often spoke of the child-poet as existing in a sort of natural harmony with primeval forces and as participating in the very sources of myth. *Le Secret professionnel* contains a parable about an ant who lived in a round bottle and who happened to be a poet:

Imaginons une fable. Des insectes enfermés dans une bouteille ronde couchée sur une table y vivent et pullulent. Au bout de quelque temps, un des insectes découvre que leur univers est plat. Quelque temps après, un autre qu'il est cubique. Quelque temps après . . . qu'ils vivent libres, mais retenus contre une surface bombée. Ainsi de suite. Un insecte, poète, écrit, pour rimer avec onde:
    Moi, pauvre prisonnier d'une bouteille ronde.
Il a tout découvert, mais il ne renseigne personne.[2]

Evidently, the "message" is that the artist's being so closely in tune with the universe allowed him to reveal its secrets. Yet in this little tale the creator did so unknowingly: seeking a word to rhyme with "onde," he fell upon "ronde" and unwittingly described his situation, because the structures of poetry correspond so closely to those of the real. Although the poet may be a vehicle through which reality manifests itself, he seems to have only partial control over it, since he does not realize the implications of what he himself has written. His privileged relationship with the cosmos and the hieroglyphs that he produces as a result gain him nothing from the point of view of mastery over his life: in addition to being a tool, an object, through which truth can enter, he himself, like his public, must decipher the code constituting his work.

When we turn to Cocteau's idealization of children as primeval artists and to his myth of redemption through art, the same phenomenon becomes evident. In *Les Enfants terribles* the "génie de la chambre" protected the children's play (in both senses of the word) and, likewise, in *Thomas l'Imposteur*, Thomas' star made it possible for him to continue. The ideal underlying both novels is that of a life which resembles a work of art, an endless series of esthetic creations somehow unconsciously perpetuated and mysteriously guarded from destruction at society's hands. In both cases, however, the continuation of the games depends not on the child's (or artist's) will but on a magical, extraordinary state. It is as if one has no choice other than to play and to hope that somehow make-believe will replace the givens of existence. In the final analysis, the artist's star rather than his desire determines his fate.

In a similar fashion, redemption in Cocteau's

mythology ultimately resides in chance. First of all,
the work of art must survive intact without being distorted in the way the Cardinal supposedly altered
Bacchus. Second, it is at the mercy of the passage of
time. Third, any heroism depicted by the poet must
be viewed as such by the public if "great disorders"
are to be vindicated. Finally, whatever victory the
work of art may represent occurs not in the creator's
lifetime but in some unspecified future. Hence, con-
quest takes place neither in contemporary history nor
in the real as commonly defined. The artist obviously
has no influence over them. For him to prevail,
legend and history must reverse their positions and
frameworks of consciousness must change: again, life
processes rather than the poet direct the course of
events. Ironically, Cocteau's "sensibilité," as Sartre
called it, led to exactly the same conclusion that the
latter had reached at the end of his intricate arguments contained in *Being and Nothingness*: the other
holds immense power because he too exists as a value-
giving consciousness, because he can make judgments,
and his perceptions about us can prevail in history no
matter how factually inaccurate they may be. Without the presence of an absolute or of an ultimate refer-
ent, each person remains, by definition, a contingent
being.

Images recurring throughout Cocteau's work only
underscore his apparent lack of control over his
environment and his pessimism about ever being able
to acquire dominance even through his art. He dotted
his conversations with references to his dependence
on the money of others. The Noailles family, for
example, gave him funds for *Le Sang d'un poète*;

Truffaut drew on profits from *Les Quatre cents coups*
for *Le Testament d'Orphée*; Madame Alec Weisweiller
kept him as a guest at her villa. The generating structures of *Le Testament d'Orphée* and of *Le Sang d'un
poète* with its divisions reminiscent of T. S. Eliot's
The Waste Land lie in evocations of trials and judgment, of miscomprehension and condemnation. At
every moment the poet exists as object and as victim.

In seeking tentative reasons for such an object-
consciousness, the critic is ultimately led to the inter-
meshing personal and social forces in Cocteau's life.
He must be cautious, however, in drawing conclusions
from these data. Although certain structures tend to
recur in many homosexual artists' works, an attempt
to link homosexuality, world view, and self-percep-
tion is a fruitless exercise. On the one hand, the
similarity between elements prevalent in Cocteau's
and Genet's creations for the stage stands out clearly:
the double, mirrors, rites, games, fantasy, and art-as-
liberation dominate each one's theater production.
Gide's art also unfolded through mirror-structures
and through an awareness of a divided self (or a self
that exists as an "other"). Yet Cocteau's homosexuality manifests itself as significant not so much in the
way it resembled that of two men with whom Cocteau has been frequently compared but, rather, in the
way it sets him apart from them. Gide and Genet
openly dealt with their homosexuality in their work:
it forms the very fabric of *Saül* and *Corydon* and is
subtly but deliberately present in *L'Immoraliste*.
Genet's fantasies pervade *Le Journal d'un voleur* and
Notre Dame des Fleurs; men play women's roles in
Les Bonnes. On the other hand, Cocteau only rarely

alluded to his sexuality in his art (the *art graphique*
being the most revealing group): his nightclub sketches
point to it clearly and he wrote love poems to Jean
Marais, but his "public" work (with the exception of
certain allusions in *Orphée* and *Les Chevaliers de la
Table ronde*—plays that can hardly be termed blatant
or militant) remains notably devoid of references to
sex. Even *Les Enfants terribles* and *Les Parents
terribles*—to whose incestuous overtones most com-
mentators have limited themselves—in essence represent possession through repression or through
prevention of the sexual act instead of through con-
sumation: they grow out of a denial of sexuality.
Gide and Genet used art as a successful exorcism for
their demons (to use Gide's term) and as a means of
coming to terms with themselves: they managed to
accommodate themselves to their fragmentation. In
Genet's *esthétique du mal*, illusion, fantasy, games,
and masks won, whereas they existed as mere pallia-
tives in Cocteau's fragile world. It seems, consequently, that homosexuality alone cannot account
for his perceptual mode. If we push one step farther
in identifying characteristics that distinguish Cocteau
from Gide and Genet, however, the role of social
identity takes on unexpected importance. What Gide
and Genet shared—as incongruous as it may appear at
first glance—and what Cocteau lacked was firm identi-
fication with a social (or, in Genet's case, an asocial)
group. Gide had very clearly received the kind of for-
mation associated with the *haute bourgeoisie*; no
preoccupation with money or social problems underlies his writings; his radical behavior was sexual rather
than political. Likewise, Genet saw himself as belong-

ing to the world of prisoners and outcasts; he had no
pretentions to being socially anything other than
what he was. Cocteau did not possess this kind of
stability: he did not inherit the amount of money
that made Gide independent, although he had the
kind of *snobisme* that made money desirable. He
apparently tried to be part of the *Tout-Paris*, but he
had to become financially dependent in order to do
so. He never clearly and unequivocably belonged to a
single social unit as a member in his own right. As a
result, his existence at all levels (rather than only one)
was insurmountably split, and his perceptions of
reality reflected a persistent fragmentation that could
not be compartmentalized or resolved.

   Out of such a world view, however, grew one of the
richest groups of creations for the stage in the
twentieth century. Cocteau's access to the major
experiments of his time made him a crossroad not
only for currents of establishment, highbrow, elite,
avant-garde, or intellectual theater but also for innova-
tions and contributions from all kinds of aural-
visual art: ballet, music-hall, cabarets, night clubs, the
Boulevard, slapstick, Charlie Chaplin, the circus.
Cocteau needed spectacle—of that there can be no
doubt, since he utilized it in every genre in which he
created—and his need resulted in an unparalleled
craftsmanship, a worship of work perfectly done.
André Breton was a rigorous, admirable theorist, but
he could not make surrealism come to life on the
stage. Having a different sort of genius—one based on
an intuition of how existence felt (rather than of how
it could be presented in argument form) and of how
it could be communicated physically so that it

reached not the mind but the emotions—Cocteau was
able to give dreams a concrete form, to incarnate
chaos or *le merveilleux* in a living, inescapable presence. It is puzzling that in discussing the evolution of
theater, historians write as if Ionesco or Genet, in the
tradition of Artaud, had alone rediscovered a tangible,
ritualistic conception of theater. Yet while no direct
connection between him and Artaud can be proven,
Cocteau was obviously the link between his work and
drama later in the century. The importance of objects, masks, movement, incantation and language in
general, evocation, associational logic, mirrors,
ambiguous representations of reality, mythic structure, the game as truth, and role playing is evident in
the plays of Ionesco and Genet, and both men ac-
knowledge their debt to him. The association of
Artaud with violent or aggressive techniques has often
obscured the fact that his ultimate aim was total
communion between audience and work, an effect
achieved by rigid codification and minute regulation
of each facet of production. Therefore, Artaud from
the point of view of theory and Cocteau from that of
success would appear to be the seminal twentieth-
century figures in redirecting theater toward its
origins in ceremony. Moreover, Cocteau's representation of man as an object in the world certainly should
not be overlooked when the art that followed him is
discussed. Many of the important issues in contemporary theater center on *mise en scène* and consequently on effective stage production. Whereas
Cocteau may not have been original in his intellec-
tualizations, he certainly was in his artisanship; his
influence resides not in his ability to say that the

individual frequently exists as an object but in his genius at making his audience feel it. More generally, within the framework of creations for the stage he could apparently create any sort of atmosphere, whether joy or terror, gaiety or sadness. In short, he was an excellent showman—a talent that should not be underrated in the realms of stage or film.

When we consider the relationship between Cocteau and his time, we must remember that according to Bernard Fay, Cocteau considered *Thomas l'Imposteur* "le premier des libres alcyoniens, gay-scienza, pieds-légers, attendus de Nietzsche."[3] The allusion "pieds légers" probably is to "The Stillest Hour" in *Thus Spake Zarathustra*: "Thoughts that come on doves' feet guide the world"[4] *The Gay Science* contains numerous quotations upon which Cocteau might have based Thomas, whom he viewed as one of the "poètes de la vie, et d'abord . . . dans les intimes banalités du quotidien."[5] In the most general sense, however, the passage in *The Gay Science* which most nearly summarizes what Cocteau wanted art and life to be is the following:

Notre derniere gratitude envers l'art.—*Si nous n'avions pas approuvé les arts, si nous n'avions pas inventé cette sorte de culte de l'erreur, nous ne pourrions pas supporter de voir ce que nous montre maintenant la Science: l'universalité du non-vrai, du mensonge, et que la folie et l'erreur sont conditions du monde intellectuel et sensible—En tant que phenomène esthétique l'existence nous reste supportable, et l'art nous donne les yeux, les mains, surtout la bonne conscience qu'il faut pour* pouvoir *faire*

3. Bernard Fay, *Les Précieux* (Paris: Librairie Académique Perrin, 1966), p. 285.
4. Walter Kaufmann, ed., *The Portable Nietzsche* (New York: Viking Books, 1969), pp. 259–260. Cf. Cocteau, *Le Rappel à l'ordre*, p. 263: "Les idées qui, disait Nietzsche, *s'avancent sur des pattes de colombes, aboutissent toujours.*"
5. Friedrich Nietzsche, *Le Gai Savoir* (Paris: Gallimard, 1950), p. 243.

6. Ibid., p. 151.

d'elle ce phénomène au moyen de nos propres
ressources. Il faut de temps en temps que nous nous
reposions de nous-memes . . .[6]

    For some scholars, it might be unthinkable to
situate Cocteau in Nietzsche's tradition: the Parisien
was too frivolous, he didn't think deeply enough, he
wasn't serious. Yet in his own way (let us remember
Sartre's remark that he had not thought Cocteau to
be as *"clown"* as his reputation would have him appear), he was indeed one of the German thinker's
most fascinating descendents, not because he reasoned
as the latter did but because he responded to many of
the same questions on a plane unlike that of Nietzsche's other admirers yet consonant with his
thought—that is, on the plane of the irrational and of
the feigned insouciance that dominated his work at
certain stages of his evolution. Gide, who was twenty
years older than Cocteau, reacted to problems of
morality and perspective in a period of evolving
values, but he seems never to have gone so far as to
imply fragmentation at the center of reality itself.
Younger men like Sartre or Camus struggled with the
absurd, with non-meaning or the destruction of
values, and ultimately channeled their reactions into
tentative answers: they attempted to "go beyond,"
as Nietzsche would say. In terms of what one might
call Nietzsche's "problem" (the situation of a human
being who was educated to believe that values preexist him and are immutable but who discovers in
the course of his life that there is no meaning), Cocteau emerges as a man who could not overcome, as
one who adopted art as escape because he could find

no other solution. His "happy," "dancing" art
represented neither a proud defiance of the absurd
nor deep joy in spite of it, but whistling in the dark
to combat fear (an image he used in *Le Secret professionnel*). He loved *spectacle* as a child would:
Genet may have disliked *L'Aigle à deux têtes* and
have called it *une belle merde* because he thought its
author was joking, but Cocteau had created it seriously. On the long path from "God is dead" to
humanity's becoming able to live happily without
gods, Cocteau remained at a starting point characterized by need and game playing. It is as if he developed
to the greatest possible extent Nietzsche's exhortation that the superior man be a poet of life, that he
give a "style" to his existence. Yet it would seem that
he himself always needed the exorcism of the art
object itself, that he could never be self-sufficient.
Only the rare child protected by a star—Thomas the
Impostor, Elizabeth and Paul in *Les Enfants terribles*—could play a game that was at once both life
and creation, and it was this primeval unity that
Cocteau sought to recapture and that Nietzsche
frequently pursued. The analogy between a child at
play and the supposed ability of primitive man to
enter completely into his own rituals, to control
the world at will so to speak, underscores Cocteau's
existential dilemma and the preeminence of theater
among forms of art with which he experimented.
For him, childhood obviously represented a period
when the self was not divided, when the distinction
between art and life did not exist, when life itself was
a perpetual act of creation. Many times, it seems as
if his art represents a desperate game, a desperate

hope that somehow make-believe will be transformed into reality and that the self can be reintegrated. The phenomenon of theater in his case takes on the aspect of a ritual in the strictest sense of the term, the structure of his life as well as his profession.

Works Cited

Apollinaire, Guillaume. "L'Esprit nouveau et les
poètes," *Mercure de de France* (December 1,
1918), pp. 385-396.

Aubarède, Gabriel d'. "Rencontre avec Jean Cocteau,"
Nouvelles littéraires, 1328 (February 12,
1953), 1, 4.

Bourdet, Denise. "Images de Paris," *La Revue de
Paris*, 66 (May 1959), 134-136.

Cocteau, Jean. "A Propos d'*Antigone*," *Gazette des
Sept Arts*, February 10, 1923.

———. "Arthur Rimbaud," *Aujourd'hui*, March 24,
1941.

———. *Le Cordon ombilical, souvenirs*. Paris: Plon,
1962.

———. *La Difficulté d'être*. Paris: Union Générale
d'Editions (Coll. 10/18), 1957.

———. *Les Enfants terribles*. Paris: Grasset, 1929.

———. *Entretien avec Roger Stéphane*. Paris: R.T.F.
et Librairie Jules Tallandier, 1964.

———. *Entretiens avec Andre Fraigneau*. Paris: Union
Générale d'Editions (Coll. 10/18), 1965.

———. *Une Entrevue sur la critique avec Maurice
Rouzaud*. Abbéville: Imprimerie F. Paillard,
1929.

———. *Essai de critique indirecte*. Paris: Grasset, 1932.

———. *Le Foyer des artistes*. Paris: Plon, 1947.

———. *L'Impromptu du Palais-Royal*. Paris: Gallimard, 1962.

———. "Une interview sur la poésie," *Conférencia*, 2 (1938), 533-549.

———. *Journal d'un inconnu*. Paris: Grasset, 1953.

———. *La Machine infernale*. Paris: Librairie Larousse [1959].

———. "Ma Pièce *L'Aigle à deux têtes* est un drame du destin," *Figaro*, April 2, 1946.

———. *Mon Premier Voyage*. Paris: Gallimard, 1936.

———. "Le Numéro Barbette," *Nouvelle Revue Française*, 27 (1926), 33-38.

———. *Opium*. Paris: Stock, 1930.

———. "Poésie, arme secret," *Le Figaro littéraire* (June 23, 1956), 1, 4.

———. *Poésie Critique I*. Paris: Gallimard, 1959.

———. *Poésie Critique II*. Paris: Gallimard, 1960.

———. "Propos sur la culture," *La Nef*, 11 (December 1955), 207-210.

———. *Rappel à l'ordre*. Paris: Stock, 1948.

———. "Secrets de beauté," *Fontaine*, 8, no. 42 (1945), 165-181.

———. *Le Secret professionnel*. Paris: Stock, 1948.

———. *Théâtre*. 2 vols., Paris: Grasset, 1957.

———. "Zola le poète," *Les Cahiers naturalistes*, 11 (1958), 442-443.

Crémieux, Benjamin. "Jean Cocteau et *La Machine infernale*," *Je Suis Partout*, April 28, 1934.

Dumesnil, René. "Phèdre à l'Opéra," in R.Supp. 3.008, Fonds Auguste Rondel, Bibliothèque de l'Arsenal.

Eliade, Mircea. *Cosmos and History*. New York: Harper and Row, 1959.

———. *Myth and Reality*. New York: Harper and Row, 1967.

———. *Myths, Dreams and Mysteries*. New York: Harper and Row, 1967.

Fay, Bernard. *Les Précieux*. Paris: Librairie Académique Perrin, 1966.

Garnier, Christine. *L'Homme et son personnage*. Paris: Grasset, 1955.

Genet, Jean. "Jean Cocteau," *Empreintes*, May-June-July, 1950.

Jung, C. G. and C. Kerenyi. *Essays on a Science of Mythology*, Bollingen Series, 22. New York:

Kaufmann, Walter, ed. *The Portable Nietzsche*. New York: The Viking Press, 1969.

Lefèvre, Frederick. *Une Heure avec . . .* Paris: Editions de la Nouvelle Revue Française, 1924.

Magnan, Jean-Marie. "La Machine à significations," *La Revue de Paris*, 72, no. 11 (1965), 42-57.

Milhaud, Darius. *"Le Pauvre Matelot et Evolution,"* *Paris-Soir*, December 9, 1921.

Nietzsche, Friedrich. *The Birth of Tragedy*. Translated by Walter Kaufmann. New York: Random House, 1967.

———. *Le Gai Savoir*. Translated by Alexandre Vialette. Coll. "Idées." Paris: Gallimard, 1950.

Oxenhandler, Neal. *Scandal and Parade. The Theater of Jean Cocteau*. New Brunswick, N.J., Rutgers University Press, 1957.

R.A. "Le Poète vit dans un rêve . . ." *Résistance-Paris-Matin*, December 21, 1946.

Sartre, Jean-Paul. "Autoportrait à 70 ans," *Le Nouvel Observateur*, 555 (June 30–July 6, 1975), 64–80.

———. *Un Théâtre de Situations*. Paris: Gallimard (Coll. "Idées"), 1973.

Taladoire, B. A. "Aux Ambassadeurs: *Les Parents terribles* de Jean Cocteau," *Cahiers du Sud* (1939), 92–96.

Touchard, Pierre-Aimé. "L'Aigle à deux têtes," *Spectateur*, February 28, 1947.

———. *Le Théâtre et l'angoisse des hommes*. Paris: Editions du Seuil, 1960.

Vivet, Jean-Pierre. "Une Reine et un anarchiste sont les héros de *L'Aigle à deux têtes* de Jean Cocteau," *Combat*, September 14, 1946.

Translations

The numbers correspond to note numbers in the text.

Chapter 2

1. Actually, the characters in a work of art are less important than its architecture. Attaching importance to a plot is equivalent to judging a painter by the models he used instead of uncovering the self-portrait which is implicit in the manner he chose to express himself.

2. half farce, half meditation on death,

4. ORPHEUS: What do we know? Who is speaking? We are stumbling around in the dark; we are in the supernatural up to our necks. We are playing hide-and-seek with the gods. We do not know anything at all.

5. THE QUEEN'S IMITATOR: Knight are you losing your mind? I get into this room after having galloped here as fast as I could, I run up the stairs four at a time and I find a judge! Poor nephew! I thought he had risen in your esteem. Please permit me to find your manner of receiving your queen and your mistress extraordinary. (S/he emphasizes the "x") May I sit down? *S/he collapses into an armchair.*

6. THE QUEEN'S IMITATOR: Keep your paws off of me. There's no contract between us that I am aware of. Nothing is eternal! I love Lancelot and I love (s/he winks as she is drinking) . . .
   LANCELOT: Galahad!
   THE QUEEN'S IMITATOR: You're the one who said his name.

7. ANUBIS: Let us obey. Mystery has its mysteries. The gods have their gods. We have ours. They have theirs. That's

what is called infinity.

8. the theater of life

9. an old theater sentimentality

10. I have been thinking for a long time about how to bring to life on a stage the atmosphere of those royal families where the desire for the art that they can never create leads them either to protect artists or, for lack of anything better, to transform their lives into lyric dramas.

11. She couldn't even count on chance, because there are lives without chance. That's my queen's style. She dreams about a fate that will come to her from outside herself, but she decides, she directs, she *gets involved with* her fate. It is probable that she is disturbing the lines of her left hand by the obsession she carries in her right hand to control everything. The problem is to know whether this is her destiny or whether she is, in fact, inventing another one for herself. That is the great enigma: The question of free will which rulers tend to confuse with their "pleasure."

12. this filthy paste

13. I think that it is getting to be difficult to tell what is dream and what is reality here.

14. In my dream, you understand, I knew that it was my poor falcon's blood.

16. The gods exist: they are the devil [or] the gods exist: that's the devil of it all.

17. Through his "reflections" (either physical or mental) the chief electrician often illuminated the play for me.

18. You never capitulated, even to the evidence.

19. That's what I called getting some gloves [or] patting oneself on the back.

20. ORPHEUS: It's a question of meaning. Listen carefully to this sentence. Listen to its mystery, "Eurydice will come back," could be just anyone, but "Madame Eurydice!" Madame Eurydice will come back—that *will* come back! That future! And then the fall: from hell.

21. a poem, a dream-poem, a flower from death's depths.

22. Madame Eurydice will come back from hell! And we refused to admit the sentence meant something.

23. blinds everybody,

24. a honeymoon wife

25. What do you expect, my dear, your head is always in the moon [clouds, in idiomatic English].

26. They enter one by one: The woman in a low-cut, red dress, very affected, very common. The red-headed woman, pretty, masculine movements, slightly bent over, her hand in her pockets. The gentleman in a velvet suit who is always looking at his wristwatch and who leaves his barstool only when he exits. A scarlet bookmaker with gold teeth who has on a gray bowler hat and a tie held in place by an enormous pearl.

27. A handsome little dead person for the next war.

28. In the case of modern plays, real language is an imitation natural language because it must seem natural.

29. It is possible that whoever invented the kaleidoscope put his finger on a huge secret. Because its infinite number of combinations grow out of three elements which on the surface have no relationship. An axis. Some pieces of glass. A mirror.

30. SECOND PHONOGRAPH: Look. The wedding party and the photographer freeze. The wedding party is immobile. Don't you find it slightly . . .
    FIRST PHONOGRAPH: Slightly senile.
    SECOND PHONOGRAPH: Slightly banquet-like.
    FIRST PHONOGRAPH: Slightly Mona-Lisa-like.
    SECOND PHONOGRAPH: Slightly masterpiece-like.

31. THE SPHINX: I speak, I work, I empty, I unroll, I calculate, I meditate, I weave, I winnow, I knit, I braid, I cross, I pass, I pass again, I knot and unknot and knot again as I hold the slightest knots that I will need to release you afterwards . . .

32. Thread, thread, thread, form your ball around my heart. Come out of me, thread, thread, thread. Thread that runs, thread that floats, Look at the profile of this prideful man. Weave your net around Renaud, thread, thread, thread.

33. Five and five no longer make ten. In the name of the monkey and of the son. In the name of the salamander. By flame and by ash. Up hill and down. Let the queen be a horse.

34. ORPHEUS: My dear you are an angel.

HEURTEBISE: Not at all.

ORPHEUS: Yes, yes, an angel, a real angel. You saved me.

35. "A sled which carries the public toward laughter or tears, in one movement, in one motion impossible to stop."

36. Look, spectator, at one of the most nearly perfect machines constructed by the infernal gods for the mathematical destruction of a mortal; a machine completely wound so that the spring unwinds slowly during a human life.

37. A mediocre victim.

38. A play by Labiche.

39. MADELEINE: If you had told me your real name . . .

GEORGE: You would have met Michael anyway.

MADELEINE: I would have avoided him.

40. the miracle of this play is that it is a vaudeville piece and a tragedy at one and the same time . . . The two are tightly linked by a double-edged fatality whose elements are coincidence and the sequence of events. A poet is capable of perceiving the meaning of these coincidences, which are not routine, when, like Cocteau, he is both humorist and playwright. Therefore, the vaudeville-like aspects of a subject can unfold at exactly the same time as the tragic ones.

41. The roles should be sacrificed to the play and should serve it rather than use it.

42. A game where large insects devour each other and are consumed.

43. Armide is dead. Do you know Renaud who is being buried? Renaud is being covered with his shield. Do you know the Renaud in the sad song? The song of Renaud, the king who is being buried. It doesn't exist yet. It should be silenced until it exists. It should be silenced. It should be silenced. Renaud's song, Renaud the King. Do you know the King Renaud, Madame? Do you know Armide?

44. I tried to write an anti-romantic romantic play whose style would be so rigorous that if the actors made a mistake with one word, they would not be able to find their balance . . .

The Eagle with Two Heads is rigorously constructed like a fugue. Edwige Feuillère, who is stunning in her strength and haughty grace, is the first theme. In the second act,

Jean Marais' theme begins. The themes come together and are separated by the articulation in Jacques Varennes' scenery. After that, the themes struggle to be resolved in the last scene where the double fall of the heroes represents this final double chord.

45. If I were inspired by any work, I would have to say that I am indebted to opera. I mean the skill of a Gluck or of a Wagner insofar as the sequence and the development of themes is concerned. *Orpheus* and *Tristan and Isolde* remain the examples of an ideal mechanism composed of long notes and short notes, of precision and of cries from the heart.

47. The play passes like an express train which is hurrying toward a final derailment.

49. The drama is treated in abbreviated form.

50. a mysterious power.

51. I planned to mix, without the slightest prudence, the actors and the characters they represented, to make a single mixture of the whole thing, comparable to the stories by Selma Lagerlöf and Lewis Carroll and to La Fontaine's fables where animals speak man's language. Because it is with tenderness that Molière declares "Actors are such bizarre animals to work with."

Chapter 3

1. The man who plays the game of art is getting involved with things that concern him at the risk of stepping out into a realm that is not his. An Einstein's discoveries surpass our small stature and do not arrive at God's feet. He (Einstein) peters out in emptiness.

2. from *Opéra* to *Renaud et Armide*, we intuit these broken temples and columns to be the visible form of a grief and of a despair which Cocteau chose to hide . . . The entire opus cracks and in these cracks anguish can be seen.

3. One must always return to Nietzsche.

4. Reimbaud and Mallarmé have become Adam and Eve. The apple is by Cézanne. We will always carry the weight of original sin.

5. We think forms, they come to life on the paper or on the canvas without having any relationship to the forms in

life. To be sensitive to the truth of forms is to understand art.

6. The poet is divided between the fear of meeting the monster and the all-devouring curiosity to see it.

7. a mass of unreconcilable contractions.

8. The poet? He is nothing other the hireling of the schizo-
phrenic which each of us carries in himself and of whom
only the poet is not ashamed.

9. a secret behavior, a discipline constructed according to the
aptitudes of a man refusing a categorical imperative, an
imperative which ruins mechanisms,

10. poetry in the rough.

11. The only excuse for the artist's existence is his taming
madness in the transcendant form of genius.

12. All children have a miraculous power to transform themselves into what they want to be. The poets in whom
childhood is prolonged suffer at the loss of this power.

13. The more or less successful exercise by which one domesti-
cates it,

14. A masterpiece is something that upsets everything, that
resembles nothing . . . and that changes the rules of
the game.

15. The spirit of creation . . . is . . . the highest form of the
spirit of contradiction,

16. Don't make art by imitating art.

17. I do not believe that someone makes progress by repeating
himself and I think that by beating on the same nail you
end up by flattening it. A single work is worth something only if it is integrated into an opus. The whole is
what counts and the repetition of a style would occasion
that boredom which commands respect and which
readers take for a fidelity to oneself, whereas it is really
only a result of boredom.

18. With each new work, I systematically turn my back on the
one that preceeded it.

19. Poetry expresses itself as it can. I refuse to put limits on it.

20. At our death, our research ceases being research; it
becomes our work.

21. I have always preferred movement to schools which make
one sit down.

22. That is the way always to begin, therefore, to remain young.

23. I do not think, therefore, I am. That's genius in a nut-shell. Thought slows down acts.

24. Barbette becomes the archetypal woman to such an extent that the beautiful young women who precede and follow him pale by comparison.

25. Great countries and civilizations gave women's roles to men not only for decency's sake . . .

26. He throws powder in one's eyes. He throws it with such force that he'll be able to think about his tight-rope act only from now on . . .

27. Because, don't forget, we are in the theater's magic light, in this malice-box where truth has no importance, where the natural has no value, where small statures become tall, tall statures become short, where card tricks and disappearing acts whose difficulty the audience doesn't even suspect are the only things that can hold up.

28. A frightful mixture of what we are and of what we are not. A trap! . . . Don't be deceived, the strange things that you are going to hear are from his pen and we have learned them.

29. We are playing a double game here . . . Dance, Sirs, in dance at the end of the strings that the invisible author is pulling above us.

30. Our profession consists in mixing the true and the false.

31. That's one hundred percent Cocteau and Louis XIV would never have thought of having such an idea.

32. My entire opus is a phenomenon of perspective. It resembles certain Dutch *troupe l'oeil*. I construct it in such a way that one can see its general meaning only from afar, in a certain light: that of death. Close up, you make out the elements that are preparing this post-humous visibility. That's why I excuse so many critics who make mistakes.

33. The poet lives in the *real* world. People are afraid of him because he puts man's nose in his excrement.

34. The forms should be that of the mind; not the manner of saying things, but of thinking them.

35. Art exists only at the moment when the artist separates himself from nature.

36. it is not in writing the word "table" that you are going to

talk about a table.

37. To paint with precision the objects that belong to the artist's world and that don't have the least connection with what people are accustomed to call reality,

38. These works are realistic only in relationship to us.

39. The truer than true,

40. In the space of an instant, we *see* a dog, a cab, a house *for the first time*. All that they have that is special, crazy, ridiculous, beautiful strikes us. Immediately afterwards, habit erases this powerful image. We stroke the dog, hail the cab, live in the house. We no longer see them.

41. ordinary objects which are recognized but transcended, seen and deciphered in a different, luxurious context which reveals the poverty of their origins and their banality.

42. One of the most disturbing forms of truth.

43. "Thibet's secret is that there isn't one and this is the secret that has to be protected before all others." This admirable sentence touched me deeply.

44. I hid the drama in the Potomak behind a thousand jokes. In the same way, one sings to keep up his courage in the dark.

45. I have often stated that a thing could not *be* and *seem* at the same time. This rule does not hold for theater, which is a place of suspicious enchantment where appearance reigns as *trompe-l'oeil* does on Italian ceilings.

46. a dream outside the head shared by us with the rest of the public,

47. A minute of contact between an audience and a work momentarily suppresses the space that separates us from other people. This phenomenon . . . permits us to live in a world where only the ritual of politeness can shelter us from the painful solitude that characterizes human beings.

48. A show which exists to bring individuals out of their separate existences and to transform them into one child-like, permeable being.

49. One evening when I had gone backstage to see Jean Cocteau at the Hebertot Theater during a showing of *The Eagle With Two Heads*, he led me into a corridor

whose doors opened out into the auditorium and he let
me observe the audience through a little opening
through which I could see them without their seeing me.
The silence was total and religious; each face was turned
toward the actors and each had the same expression
of engrossed interest and deep empathy. 'For me,'
Cocteau said, 'seeing them like that is the greatest joy I
derive from working in theater.' The elderly poet was
indeed particularly sensitive to this stunning magic
created by theater, a magic that unites people who have
come together by chance into such a feeling of communion with the characters that they all feel the same joys
and the same sorrows with the same intensity.

50. Poetry in general is a precision instrument.

53. a logical unfolding of illogical circumstances

Chapter 4

4. a thirst for unreality,

5. We must insist again that none of the protagonists in this
theater and even the one who was filling the spectator's
role was aware of playing a part. The play owed its
eternal youth to this primitive lack of awareness. Without their even suspecting it, the play (or the bedroom if
you wish) was poised on the edge of myth.

6. a myth is a myth because poets use it again and again and
prevent it from dying.

8. This childhood from which I will never escape,

9. Childhood was the only happy period of my life.

10. *The greatest change.* Lighting and colors have all changed!
We no longer understand very well how primitive men
perceived the most ordinary things—daybreak and
awakening, for example; since they believed in dreams,
the period spent awake had a different meaning for
them than it does for us . . . Everything had a different
light about it, because a god was shining in it; all
decisions and all long-term plans were different, too,
because men had oracles, they had secret warning
systems and people believed in the power of predictions.
"Truth" was perceived differently, because the madman
was the person who deciphered it. What joy must have
been like at a period when people believed in the devil,
in the temptor . . .

11. When you hear it said of an artist or of a woman that he
or she is "angelical," don't expect to find the images of
an angel that you had at your first communion.

A lack of self-interest, egoism, tender pity, cruelty,
suffering at physical contact, purity in debauchery,
coexistence of a violent taste for the pleasures of the
earth and scorn for them, naive amorality, don't be
deceived: these are the signs of what we call angelism;
each true poet has these signs, whether he writes, paints,
sculpts or sings. Few persons are capable of this, but
few people can feel poetry.

12. it thinks only of its belly and of an invisible task whose
visible side underscores its total indifference to
individual suffering.

13. A young, charming, vigorous, stunning animal.

14. Using this principle, I wrote that Genet is a moralist and
that "I am a lie that always tells the truth," a sentence
which idiots managed to transform into something
ridiculous because that's what they wanted to hear. The
sentence meant that man is socially a lie. The poet
tries to fight social lies especially when they exist to
destroy what he is as an individual and when they
accuse him a being a lier. There is nothing harsher than
this defense of the masses at the expense of the individual. Parrots everywhere repeat "the poet is lying," when
actually he tries never to lie.

15. Whether I am the son of the muses or of a chimney sweep,
I will know things.

16. THE SHEPHERD: You are the son of Jocasta, your wife,
and of Laius whom you killed at the point where three
roads come together. Incest and parricide, may the gods
forgive you.
    OEDIPUS. I killed the man I should not have killed. I
married the woman I should not have married. I perpetuated what should not have been perpetuated. I
now understand.

17. JOCASTA: Yes, my child, my little child . . . If you only
knew what little importance all those things have that
humans find abominable when they are seen from where
I am now.

18. One should never confuse the night about which I am
speaking and the one into which Freud invited his

patients. Freud burgled pitiful apartments. He managed to get some erotic pictures out of them. He never honored the abnormal in its status of something transcendent. He never paid homage to the great disorders.

19. I want to know and I will know . . .

20. I must take responsibility for my acts.

21. The reign of truth is about to begin. It is harsh. It will be painful at the start.

22. One must always pay. Pay with himself and with his acts.

24. I thought that life was like the picture on a postcard. I didn't understand at all. Now I do.

25. There are forces that push us toward catastrophe.

26. The rest of the role is that of a woman made for love, a woman who is awkward and noble. At the end, she has "learned a lot." *She remembers her roles.* Her sincerity is slightly colored by the theater.

27. The end fitting a farce after five months of tragic torture.

28. To me, *The Terrible Parents* is purity itself. There is a closed atmosphere where evil does not enter, where the question of good and evil isn't even asked. This is what links the play to the novel *The Terrible Children*.

29. LEO: I am not mean. I have been observing you since yesterday, Yvonne, and I congratulate myself for having brought some order into the trailer. In this world, there are children and adults. Unfortunately, I'm one of the adults and you others belong to the race of children who never stop being children and who would commit crimes . . .

30. MADELEINE: I hate lies. The smallest lie makes me sick. I accept the fact that someone might be quiet so that things work out with as few complications as possible. But real lying. . . a lie that is a simple luxury! I am not really being moral, because, in fact, I am quite amoral. I intuit that lies upset processes which transcend us and that they upset waves, that they get everything out of joint.

31. There are houses and lives whose existence would stupify reasonable people.

32. The spirit of the room was watching,

33. It was the theme of the solitude of human beings who sense each other's presence when neither is visible but

who cannot manage to join each other when they are visible.

34. "all saints refuse to obey existing laws and that is why they are tortured."

35. I approached the theme of confusion among youth surrounded by different dogmas and sects and frustrated by obstacles. Vulnerable to offers of service and to emotion, they seek to remain free. Their freedom helps them make their way among obstacles until the latter destroy them. They can overcome opposition only through ruse or through a seizing of power. The skill that deviousness requires is lacking, however. Young people rush forward. Their awkward purity, their audacity, their hearts, their senses are all a disservice to them in a society where deviousness reigns and where indirect lines cross each other . . .

37. Yvonne is a fire which is devouring itself.

38. He plays loser-takes-all whereas those who serve the visible can only play a game in which the winner ultimately loses.

40. a masterpiece of horror.

41. Your police have been well trained, Creon, but where this man is, they don't have the least power.

42. TIRESIAS: They no longer belong to you: you have no further power over them.
    CREON: To whom do they belong, then?
    TIRESIAS: To the people, to poets and to those who are pure of heart.

44. I hope to charm real beasts one day,

45. It is probable that poets' work is like planting seeds, that it is a form of work much closer to nature than people think; it is the kind of work plants do. The seeds fall where they can; some grow and some do not.

47. You have to assassinate quickly and outside. You have to assassinate quickly and then be stoned by the crowd. If not, then the level of drama falls and anything that loses its intensity is unbearable.

Chapter 5

1. For example, I liked Cocteau, whom I met in 1944 and whom I saw frequently up until the time of his death.

I had dinner with him a few days before he died. I liked him a great deal and I thought him to be much less of a jester than he is usually portrayed to be now.

He was the one who talked. He talked about the way he saw the world and about his ideas—I really couldn't follow him very well because in my opinion he was superficial. He was a brilliant conversationalist, he was sensitive, but he was not a man of ideas. That does not mean, however, that I do not consider him a great poet.

2. Let's imagine a fable. Some insects live closed up in a bottle found lying on a table. After a while, one of the insects finds out that their universe is flat. Later, another discovers that it is three-dimensional. Later, one proposes that they are free but trapped next to a convex surface. One insect, who is a poet, writes the following line in order that it rime with the word *onde* (wave): "I, poor prisoner in a round *(ronde)* bottle." He has revealed everything, but he has informed no one.

3. The first of the gay-science-like, light-footed books awaited by Nietzsche.

5. poets of life and first of all in the ordinary things that happen every day.

6. *Our last gratitude toward art.* If we had not accepted the arts, if we had not invented this cult of error, we would never be able to stand what present-day science shows us: the universality of non-truth, of lies; madness and error are the conditions under which the life of the mind and of the senses is lived. As an esthetic phenomenon, existence remains bearable, and art gives us the eyes, the hands, and especially the good conscience one has to have in order to transform life into something on the level of our capacities. From time to time, we have to take a rest from ourselves.

Index